A SURVIVAL HANDBOOK
FOR THE
SCHOOL LIBRARY
MEDIA SPECIALIST

A Survival Handbook for the School Library Media Specialist

Betty Martin

Library Professional Publications   1983

Library of Congress Cataloging in Publication Data

Martin, Betty, 1910-
　A survival handbook for the school library media specialist.

　Bibliography: p.
　Includes index.
　1. School libraries—Handbooks, manuals, etc.
　2. Instructional materials centers—Handbooks, manuals, etc.
　3. Libraries—Psychology—Handbooks, manuals, etc.
　4. Educational innovations—Handbooks, manuals, etc.
　I. Title
　Z675.S3M2737　1983　　　　025.5'678　　　　83-14851
　ISBN 0-208-02047-0
　ISBN 0-208-01997-9 (pbk.)

©1983 Betty Martin. All rights reserved.
First published as a Library Professional Publication,
an imprint of The Shoe String Press, Inc.,
Hamden, Connecticut 06514

Printed in the United States of America

Contents

Foreword	vii
Introduction	1
1. Stress	5
2. Some Basic Survival Strategies	17
3. Employer-Sponsored Stress-Reduction Programs	26
4. Interpersonal Relations	34
5. Relations with Administrators	38
6. Relations with Teachers	45
7. Relations with Students	51
8. Relations with Parents and Community Members	56
9. The Dynamics of Change	62
10. New Technologies	67
11. Changes in the Student Body	78
12. Changes in the Curriculum and School Organization	88
13. Changes in Financial Support	96
Summary of Stress-Survival Strategies	106
Appendixes	109
Bibliography	133
Index	145

Foreword

The role of the library media specialist in the schools has undergone a drastic change over the past two decades. During this time school libraries have become complete instructional media centers, with librarians responsible for administering nonprint collections and accompanying hardware and often production and video units in addition to constantly growing collections of print materials. Even more significant, the responsibility of the library media specialist has shifted and expanded in scope: from merely organizing and supplying materials to supplement or enrich learning, the library media specialist has moved rapidly to prescribing materials as integral components of the learning program, and beyond that to assisting with the design of the curriculum itself.

Now these same practitioners are facing a future which will require that they perform in a society operated by high technology. As schools become larger and programs more diverse, there are demands upon the library media specialist to serve both teachers and students in new ways, often without adequate staff for doing so. Pressures from within and without have mounted, and will continue to mount. Parents request additional services and question programs, materials and the expertise of the professional staff. The community demands accountability, and the majority of the population that supports the schools but has no children in them increases rapidly. Budgets are diminishing to the extent that media centers stand to lose ground at a time when they should be in a position to take leadership in the use of the new technology and become active participants in resource networks.

For some media specialists the changes have been traumatic; they have been unable to make the transition and have left the profession. Others have begun to doubt that their training has been adequate for them to continue in this new field. The ones who remain are looking to all sectors for assistance.

This book by Betty Martin addresses itself to "coping" for the library media specialists. It is alive with the author's own forward-looking philosophy which has made her a successful practitioner for over thirty years. The importance to the library media program of good human relations cannot be overestimated. Abrasive personal relations can negate an otherwise good library media program by "turning off" students and teachers, while good public relations can improve an average program. Help is here for improving relations with students and teachers, administrators and parents. Such a book has been needed, and it should be welcomed equally by the novice and by the more experienced library media specialist.

Margaret W. Ehrhardt
Library/Media Consultant
South Carolina Department
of Education

Introduction

There are many factors in the library media specialist's daily life which have the potential of causing tension and stress, and this book addresses two that seem the most culpable: changes in the environment, and the ongoing daily friction of interpersonal relations—in large part worsened by environmental changes.

Those of us in the educational world have become very much aware of change, and even quite knowledgeable about it. We know that it is inevitable and accelerating. We have accepted the fact that new technologies will create enormous changes in the way we live and do our work. But although this hardware would seem threatening enough, it can't compare with the stress potential of the social, economic and political changes that have already shown themselves, and with uncertainty about the values and standards of the future. Most stressful of all for school people, perhaps, are the shifts in family attitudes about education, about freedom of speech and expression, and about teachers and librarians as advocates of the free flow of information, open minds and individual choices.

We know also that some planned change is desirable, and we have become familiar with the role of the change agent. But planned or not, we realize that change is a constant in our lives. No one can know, of course, exactly what education and libraries will be like in the year 2050, but the present rates of growth in technology, and demographics—including the sizes of generations already born and population movements—can help us predict and project with some probable degree of accuracy. It may well be, for example, that professionals with training similar to that of today's school library media specialists will be working out of regional continuing education centers, large complexes serving a population of a hundred thousand people of all ages in large part through interactive cable into their homes.

The changes of the next fifty years or so will demand a great deal of all human beings, not only school librarians and other educators, of course. In the natural world, plants, animals, birds and insects all experience and adapt to environmental changes in habitat, climate and food or water supply. This adaptation in response to change requires many years, often hundreds of them. School library media specialists, in common with other professionals and other humans generally, do not, unfortunately, have the luxury of many years to adapt to immense changes.

Because things are happening so fast, reaction to the impact is apt to be negative—often in the extreme. At the present time reactions may include a stiff upper lip and dug-in heels, and the grim vow *not* to change procedures and programs; or even if there is no overt hostility, there may be apathy, or an attempt to muddle through while feeling threatened and tense, to the accompaniment of ulcers, migraines and a host of other stress symptoms.

Some few, of course, will embrace all change in the status quo for its own sake, and without thought or discrimination. This is no more desirable than outright resistance to all change, but there is a middle road. In taking it, one views changes within the framework of the purposes and objectives of the library media program, and considers the possibility provided for each student to develop the broadest base for lifetime learning and enjoyment of ideas in any format. Those who have become recognized as measured and thoughtful in their acceptance of changes in the school library media program—or in any aspect of the learning program as a whole, for that matter—need not hesitate to reject proposed changes that are specious and undesirable.

Persons under stress in any setting—a home, a school, a business office or any other—can wreak havoc upon each other. The nature of the library media program in the school necessitates frequent communication and collaboration with many diverse groups: students, teachers, administrators, parents and other community members. Unless the library media specialist has highly developed interpersonal skills based on a stable and confident self-identity and a positive professionalism, it is quite likely that discords and disagreements will occur. It is crucial, therefore, that library media specialists learn good coping strategies that will enable them to absorb, meet, or in some cases turn aside pressures, and prevent the development of tension and stress. The school library media specialists in today's and tomorrow's school building can gain and utilize enormous influence and leadership by so doing.

The purpose of this book is to help them in this endeavor. After focusing on present and projected change that will vitally affect education and the work of the library media specialist, and on the impact of these changes on interpersonal relations, some strategies for survival—even triumphant survival—are suggested.

Underlying all of this is a basic agreement with the premise expressed by Arnold Brown(23)*: "People don't have to be afraid of the future.... Most of us are quite adaptable, particularly when necessity twists our arms.... Now we are moving into an age where power resides not in size or weapons or property but in information. The people who control information, control access to it, control understanding of it, control interpretation of it, are the people who will be the gatekeepers of power in the new age."

Come what may, those who will work in the library information field of the future will have an inside track.

*Numbers in parentheses refer to the numbered bibliography.

1
STRESS

According to the dictionary the word *stress* may refer to either an effect or a cause, as: 1) physical, mental or emotional tension, and/or 2) a situation or factor causing this. Although in recent years stress (as effect) has been perceived to be endemic to the teaching profession, frequently escalating into the condition known in popular terms as "burnout," it also may plague many other types of professional people—especially those who deal constantly with problems, such as doctors and social workers—as well as executives, athletes, housewives and, increasingly, school-age children and teen-agers. Many school library media specialists are similarly afflicted.

Anderson defines stress as cause: "any stimulus, real or imagined, which requires an individual to be or to do anything different from the way he is or the way he behaves at any given moment. . . . Stress is any stimulus which demands adaptation on the part of the organism involved"(4).

Seyle emphasizes that "Stress is the *nonspecific* response of the body to any demand"(127). He states that the stress-producing factor, or stressor, as it is called, may be pleasant or unpleasant—a broken finger, a game of chess, a kiss—and the nonspecific response, or systemic reaction, will be the same. However, the *specific* reactions may be quite different or completely opposite. "Damaging or unpleasant stress is 'distress.'"

We are told that stress is not merely nervous tension, and that it cannot be entirely avoided. While you are alive there is the need to meet demands and to adapt to changing external influences. "Complete freedom from stress is death." Most of us probably realize that if stress is not extreme, or more distressful than merely stressful, it operates as a motivating factor and impels us to overcome, to adapt or to achieve.

Stress on the job Checklist(155)
There are conditions at work which are often stressful. On the items below, indicate how stressful each item is for you:

$$1 = \text{Never}$$
$$2 = \text{Seldom}$$
$$3 = \text{Sometimes}$$
$$4 = \text{Often}$$
$$5 = \text{Always}$$

____ 1. I am unclear about what is expected of me on the job.
____ 2. Others' demands for my time at work are in conflict.
____ 3. Commuting to and from work is a constant headache.
____ 4. "Management" expects me to interrupt my work for new priorities.
____ 5. I have a poor relationship with my supervisor.
____ 6. I only receive feedback when my performance is unsatisfactory.
____ 7. There is little chance for promotion within my organization.
____ 8. Decisions or changes which affect me are made from above without my knowledge or involvement.
____ 9. I have to work under crowded and noisy conditions.
____ 10. I have too much to do and too little time to do it.
____ 11. I feel uncomfortable with the political climate of the organization.

___ 12. I do not have enough work to do.
___ 13. The fear of failure is constantly on my mind.
___ 14. I feel over-qualified for the work I actually do.
___ 15. I feel under-qualified for the work I actually do.
___ 16. I feel pressures from home about my work hours.
___ 17. I spend my time fighting fires rather than working on a plan.
___ 18. The organization with which I work is continually threatened by layoffs.
___ 19. I don't have the opportunity to use my knowledge and skills on the job.
___ 20. It seems I move from one deadline to another.

Clearly, the higher your total score, the heavier the burden of stress you are carrying.

School library media specialists may be particularly vulnerable to stress due to two major aspects of their work:

There have been many recent changes in the nature and scope of their work which require new practices and programs, and there is a certainty of many more changes to come; and

Their work requires many contacts and diverse types of interpersonal relationships which have the potential for causing distress.

Both of these pressures will be fully addressed in the following chapters.

What are the effects of these and other pressures? Walsh describes them(146):

A reaction of the nervous system to stress, leading to a variety of physical diseases.

A disruption of personal or professional life as a result of occupational stress.

Destructive feelings of emotional stress as a result of ineffective coping.

Loss of concern and detachment from those with whom you work.

A cynical and dehumanized perception of students, accompanied by a deterioration of the quality of teaching.

These effects may manifest themselves in a number of different ways. If your answer must be "yes" to one or more of the following questions, and you have these feelings on a continuing and not just an occasional and transitory basis, they are symptoms of stress:

Do you dread to get up in the morning?
Do you feel emotionally and physically exhausted?
Do you have a sense of low self-esteem?
Do you feel a lack of commitment?
Are you unable to cope?
Are you anxious and depressed?
Do you feel that you've lost control of a situation?
Do you feel that your work is deteriorating?
Do you feel frustrated?
Do you long to get away from it all?

Extreme stress of long duration can result in high blood pressure, migraine headaches, severe depression, heart disease, ulcers, colitis and many other ills, both mental and physical.

Jones and Emanuel describe the three stages a teacher goes through during the development of stress(75):

1. Heating-up stage—feelings of dissatisfaction and isolation, belief that personal efforts are not appreciated, underlying feelings of rejection, little positive reinforcement received, a fading zest for teaching;
2. Boiling stage—pangs of helplessness felt, usefulness as a teacher questioned, other occupations look more prestigious, belief that any challenging efforts are stifled or ignored;
3. Explosion stage—covert responses may include becoming a robot, using notes and assignments not revised for years, being apparently unaffected by environment, performing mechanically required teach-

ing tasks; overt responses may include fighting feelings by leaving the profession, or engaging in open rebellion against the whole teaching structure.

When a person's stress becomes full-blown his or her response varies and can be triggered or modified by various factors. Abrego and Brammer list three of these factors(2):

1. Cultural differences. For example: if you were reared in a culture and in a family which strongly emphasized the work ethic, this would influence your relationship with misbehaving students who apparently have no such commitment.
2. The quality of the stress event. This quality, associated with change, would affect your reaction depending upon whether the event is less stressful or more stressful:

less stressful	*more stressful*
predictable	unpredictable
voluntary	involuntary
familiar	unfamiliar
of low magnitude (the degree of change)	of high magnitude
of low intensity (rate of change)	of high intensity

Example: a library media specialist from a conventional library media center who was suddenly transferred to a school with an "open" library media center would probably suffer great stress.

3. The strength of support systems. These consist of both internal and external supports. Part of the internal supports are self-messages we give ourselves. They may be self-defeating, as:

"I've never liked to be around people who are different. I just can't work with physically disabled students."

"I've never been any good in math. I can't help plan a new unit in this area of the curriculum."

"New technology is a mystery to me. It makes me feel stupid. I can't learn to operate that microcomputer."

"I'm just not an outgoing person, and I'm not going to work with people I don't like. I can't establish good relationships with all the teachers."

These positive messages to self might be self-enhancing instead:

"I've learned new things before, and I can do it again."

"This is a challenge. If I can learn this it will be a personal as well as a professional accomplishment."

"This is going to be stimulating. I would like to have some new skills."

"It will broaden my experience to become friendly with the different kinds of people who are teachers here."

External supports include contacts with people with whom you share common interests, people who have had similar experiences and can make you feel competent and valued. You need actively to seek out people who can give you information and who will share your concerns and feelings in a constructive way.

Pauline Anderson, a leader among independent school library media specialists, and Director of the Andrew Mellon Library at the Choate-Rosemary Hall School in Wallingford, Connecticut, provided a round-up of pressures on the school library media program and those who direct it, in the Connecticut Educational Media Association's newsletter, *Update*. She characterizes as "internal" pressures those developing within the library media center itself, and the "external" pressures as those that emanate from the total school environment and the wider community as well as the society in general. Ms. Anderson also identifies some support systems, and some strategies for coping with pressures, subjects with which we shall deal in the following chapters.

COPING WITH PRESSURE ON THE SCHOOL LIBRARY MEDIA PROGRAM

Pressures on school library media programs present themselves in many shapes, sizes and forms—some tangible and some intangible. Pressures differ from school to school; pressures which place major constraints on the program of one library media center program may be non-existent in another library media center. As individuals responsible for school library media programs we cannot predict with unerring accuracy the identity of every pressure which will arise but we can identify with almost absolute accuracy the potential sources of pressures.

The process of identifying the potential sources of pressure is neither endless nor tedious. As one starts to chart the broad categories of potential sources (see accompanying chart) one discovers quickly that the categories march single file and of their own accord onto the chart. Surprises are simply not forthcoming for the categories are all ones we recognize but may never have organized. Preparing a chart which identifies all potential sources of pressure is the first and most essential step in a well-developed plan for coping. As Thomas Mann warned in *The Magic Mountain*, "The actual enemy is the unknown." A visible chart converts the potential enemy from an unknown to a known quantity.

The obvious question which arises when one looks at the completed chart is, "How do I cope with these pressures—individually and collectively?" The single and vastly oversimplified answer is "to build support systems." The degree of oversimplification in this answer depends upon individual definitions of support systems. If one's definition of a support system is broad—ranging from the very simple to the complex—one can put into place with relative ease a number of support systems to help cope. Many support systems are already in place but may have never been identified by this terminology.

Support systems are our insurance policies—available when we need them. A support system can be something as simple as a single quotation such as the remark made by the U.S. Commissioner of Education, Harold Howe, in 1967, "What a school thinks about a library is a measure of what it thinks about education." A quotation from a highly-respected educator can be a powerful instrument when used at the appropriate moment in the appropriate setting. If one is working with administrators on long-range plans, Blanche Woolls's article, "Where Will Your Library Media Center Be In 1985," in the April, 1982 issue of the *National Association of Secon-*

dary School Principals Bulletin provides support. Statistics on a single issue—whether the issue deals with budget, staffing, open hours or something more esoteric—garnered from comparable school library media centers offer effective support for many kinds of pressures.

Clearly articulated and written policies are our major allies. If a Policy for Handling Controversial Materials and the appropriate forms for follow-up action are ready to be distributed to the would-be censor, the issue can be handled as a routine matter and not be an instantaneous pressure point. Even though the individual case may eventually become a major issue, the plan of action is ready. If a Gift Policy which includes a statement on procedures for dealing with appraisals is available to donors, the donor who anticipates a large tax deduction in return for fifty useless books will no longer be a bugaboo. Widely distributed Disaster Preparedness Plans which detail priorities for action when disaster strikes make the sound of the fire or water alarm less threatening. Each of us should be aware of the services available from the New England Document Conservation Center (NEDCC) in Andover, Massachusetts. A Disaster Preparedness Plan should include the telephone number and emergency services available from the NEDCC.

All pressures are not disasters or emergencies. Some pressures result from lack of time and many of these can be averted by careful planning. The opening days of every new academic year resemble a fast-moving merry-go-round. Returning teachers and students, familiar with our services, resources and procedures, are ready for action. New teachers and new students can easily become lost to us during the hectic opening days. However, if before school opens (preferably in the preceding spring term) a letter goes from the head of the school library media center to every incoming new teacher, a bridge will already have been built by the opening day of the academic year. Tell the new teacher about available services and resources, urge that individual to visit the center before school opens and indicate staff availability for discussions. If annual spring term planning for the next academic year includes an opening day's time slot for orientation of new students, another pressure has been removed and allows one to concentrate on the program rather than trying to find time for the program.

A support system can be a group of persons—chosen from far and/or near. Fellow professionals from a variety of school library media centers and other kinds of libraries can often lighten our real or imagined burdens and can always lift our spirits. These persons should be carefully identified for their varying and unique expertise. Existing groups within our building or system often function as excellent support systems. Well-informed department chairpersons can be among our greatest supports. A student or parent group may exist which would welcome some type of constructive school library media center role. If no groups currently exist which can offer needed support, organize one or more to fulfill different functions.

As part of our long-range plan for coping with pressures we can look beyond our immediate home territory and identify a number of groups and organizations which are 'out there' with support systems already in place and eager to help. Our professional library media organizations—national, regional and state, professional organizations of other disciplines such as the National Council of Teachers of English, the Office of Intellectual Freedom, the Freedom to Read Foundation, the Society of American Archivists, the Connecticut Association of Independent Schools and countless other organizations are among our friends.

We in Connecticut are fortunate to have able consultants at the state level on whom we can call. We in Connecticut are fortunate also that our State Board of Education has had the foresight and the wisdom to be the first state to adopt 'Free to Learn,' a policy on academic freedom and public education.

As we look again and again at the chart we have prepared we discover that it is possible to have numerous support systems in place to help us cope with the many kinds of pressures which can affect our programs. One of the most pleasant truths we learn from the chart is that imaginative pre-planning will prevent many pressures from arising. The most unpleasant truths we learn are that some pressures arise because we professionals do not, on occasion, pay sufficient attention to detail, fail to establish realistic priorities, or neglect to plan thoroughly. In these instances we have to be our own support system! As we realize that our own role within the school is one of leadership and support rather than the outdated view which assigned us only a support role, the enormity of some pressures evaporates. As we cope more effectively with pressures within the school library media center our programs will prosper and expand, our students will benefit, our colleagues will rejoice and relax with us. We must, in the words of Homer, "Learn calm to face what's pressing."

SOURCES OF PRESSURE

Internal	External
HUMANS	
Library Users	Alumni
Library Staff	Boards of Education
Colleagues	Trustees
Administrators	Parents
	Parent Groups
	Donors
	Friends of the Library
	Members of Community
RESOURCES	
Print	Gifts
Non-Print	Museums
Special Collections	Libraries
Equipment	Public
	Special
	Academic
	State
	Historical Societies
	Networks
	Consortia
FINANCES	
Budgets	Fund Raising
Operating	Capital Drives
Capital	Foundation Grants
Personnel	Private Grants
Endowment	Federal Grants
Special Funding for	State Grants
New Programs	Sponsored Events
EVALUATION	
Personnel	State
Program	Regional (NEASC)
PROFESSIONALISM	
Status	Which professional organizations are most appropriate for institutional support and personal participation in terms of time, money, benefits and workshops?
Committees	
Academic Policy	
Curriculum Committee	
Faculty Committees	
Self Image	
Library Image	

Internal	External
USE OF LIBRARY 　　Academic Use vs. 　　Study Hall or Social Center	Student/Parent Alumni Functions
COMMUNICATION 　　Constant effort to effect 　　total school awareness of 　　resources and program	Constant effort to effect total community awareness of resources and program
ROLE 　　Leadership 　　Support 　　Academic Department 　　Interdisciplinary 　　Department	Necessity or Luxury

OTHER SOURCES OF PRESSURE

ARCHIVES
　　Archival collection Vs.
　　Library Collection

CONSERVATION AND
PRESERVATION
　　Resources
　　Energy

LEGISLATION
　　Copyright Law & Guidelines
　　Thor Decision
　　IRS (gifts, appraisals)
　　Federal Grants
　　State Grants
　　OSHA
　　State Propositions

SOCIETY
　　Impact of TV
　　Moral Majority
　　Creationists
　　Vandalism and Theft
　　Inflation
　　In Loco Parentis
　　Information Explosion
　　Declining Birthrate
　　Walkman Tape Recorders

ADMINISTRATION
　　Establish, design and
　　implement:
　　Priorities
　　Policies
　　Programs
　　Support Systems

MAINTENANCE
　　Daily and long term upkeep
　　and maintenance of
　　Building-including systems
　　such as heating and air
　　cond. Equipment

SPACE
　　Organization of space
　　Reorganization of space
　　Long term planning for space
　　Designing New Space

TECHNOLOGIES
　　Which of the newer tech-
　　nologies are appropriate, useful
　　and affordable for my library?

EDUCATIONAL PROGRAM
　　Curriculum
　　On campus cultural, recrea-
　　tional and political happenings.

Pauline Anderson. Reprinted by permission from the Connecticut Educational Media Association *Update* Fall, 1982.

Possession of coping skills is of the greatest importance. Library media specialists need to develop new behavioral responses to cope with new situations and thus limit and relieve stress. The following chapters discuss planned responses and strategies.

As we proceed with the investigation of how to minimize the stress of school library media work and thus survive now and in the future, it might be well to bear in mind an affirmation that appears, expressed in different ways, in the writings of Marcus Aurelius, Saint Francis and Reinhold Niebuhr, among others:

> I feel determined to strive to use whatever power I have to change the unpleasant stresses of life that I can change, to dislike but realistically accept those I cannot change, and to have the wisdom to know the difference between the two.

2
Some Basic Survival Strategies

Although library media specialists are susceptible to attacks of stress, they are strategically situated to react to it positively rather than negatively. They are committed in their work with others in the school community to an important cause: the intellectual and personal development of children and young people, and so, quite directly, to the enhancement of a democratic society. They serve this cause by creating, with others, a pleasant, productive learning environment and stimulating learning opportunities for individuals and groups. The very nature of their work is positive and ego-satisfying, for they are providing young people with mind-expanding choices, opening to them horizons and vistas.

School library media specialists have, in most cases, built up a reservoir of goodwill, appreciation and respect from many past experiences. In this situation, they are in a better position than most people to follow Seyle's guidelines for facing stressors encountered in the fight to survive(127):

1. Find your own natural predilections and stress level. Engage in planned self-analysis to establish what you really want in order to ensure your future fulfillment and happiness.

2. Practice altruistic egoism. Hoard the esteem, goodwill and love of those with whom you are associated.
3. Be conscious of the things you do that earn love, and do them.

We would add to this last, conversely, avoid doing those things which promote tension, fear or diminution in others.

If you ignore this advice and if your response to stress is a decision to withdraw into your shell and try to ignore the changes going on around you as well as the friction in your relations with others in the school community, you have made an unwise choice. You will become a problem and a stumbling block, hampering the efforts of your colleagues and condemning your students to a learning environment weakened and marred by deteriorating human relations.

Let us hope that you will opt to mobilize your personal response to stress, a course that will doubtless bring you strength and stimulation for meeting future strains and a great feeling of being able to cope. In addition, your students will benefit from the changes which your resolution of stress has enabled you to help make in a creative atmosphere free of dissension and discord. You will find that the positive effort you are making will bring you the admiration and respect of most of your colleagues, and, even more importantly enhance your own self-respect.

In planning a positive response pattern there are two factors to be considered: internal and external. The internal factor which has the most effect upon your response to stress is your attitude. You attitude toward an event has an important relationship to your interpretation of that event. Examine carefully and honestly your attitude toward change and toward your interpersonal relations. You will save yourself much grief if you can develop an attitude of acceptance: acceptance both toward change and toward a normal amount of the disruption and dislocation that change brings about. Approach problems with the attitude that they *can* and *will* be resolved. The key attribute here is flexibility. Flexible attitudes toward personal relations, toward instructional practices, toward curricular changes and school organization will help obviate distress produced by stressful situations. Stress hits hardest and most disagreeably at the rigid, inflexible person.

Also in the area of internal factors is the need to maintain a realistic view of yourself and your own behavior. You may perceive that you are outgoing, that you accept others as they are and as worthy humans beings, that you are warm, approachable and helpful to others. But be painfully honest. Do you resent criticism? Are you apt to hold grudges? Do you have poor leadership qualities? Do you lack assertiveness? Are you afraid to stand by your own convictions, or, standing by them fearlessly, do you fail sometimes to remember that you could be wrong?

It takes a good deal of courage and a conscious effort to evaluate one's strengths and weaknesses. You cannot concentrate on eliminating the thorns you present to the sides of others until you have identified them.

Abrego and Brammer advise strengthening internal support systems with what they characterize as "self-talk." These are both the lectures we give ourselves and the thoughts and feelings that run, often unbidden, through our minds, such as "I can't handle this situation;" "This kind of person always intimidates me," or "I have the competence and experience to handle this." Being conscious of this "self-talk" and being able to evaluate it, one can restructure the negative to design positive statements that will bolster self-esteem. It might help to keep a journal of a day's "self-talk" for a period of several days, evaluate it, and try changing it into positive statements that will bolster your self-esteem and propel you in a forward direction instead of sideways or backwards! Some examples of this kind of internal strategy were given in the previous chapter.

Another suggestion in this internal area is that you learn relaxation skills. If you allow yourself to get tense about a situation, it is very hard to remain calm, self-assured and in control of either yourself or the situation. Much has been written about this subject, and you can consult the literature, or you may request your school district consultant for personnel or guidance services to conduct a workshop for you and your media staff on relaxation skills. (See Appendix A for material about relaxation therapy.)

The principal external factors in your plan for a positive response pattern to stress are a detailed plan for action and a program of continuing education or group therapy of one kind or another. In fact, sharing and cooperation with others is essential.

Since we assumed before discussion of the internal factors that you have rejected the negative response—that of withdrawing, doing nothing, complaining or blaming others and otherwise hugging to yourself the feeling that you are sinking fast—it is time, at this point, to examine the options for external action.

First, it is useful to list in priority order the tasks to be performed. Examine the positive and negative consequences of alternatives, search for relevant information, and then make a detailed plan to implement the chosen alternative. Identify skills needed: overcoming shyness, leading discussions, accepting the ideas of others and the like.

Discuss your sense of need and plans for meeting it with a close friend—probably a professional colleague who will understand your problems—or perhaps with the district library media services director or an understanding and supportive principal. Involve your immediate staff (if you have one) in the planning. Discuss interpersonal relations with them, and problem solving. Open up channels of communication so that you and those you talk to can begin to stop feeling "bottled up."

You may want to begin with consideration of a well-planned program of continuing professional education for yourself and your staff, or other members of your faculty. Accept, and help others to accept, the fact that making the effort to keep on learning is an important step in getting control of the situation that is causing stress and your own reactions to it. As Daniel says, "To see the role of the school media specialist as really professional can be somewhat frightening without the concomitant attitude that professional development means lifelong learning. One never knows enough"(39). And, one might add, the more one knows the more secure one feels, and the less vulnerable.

Professional education activities can be expected to give you some clues about working with teachers. The following is one example of active planning in a stressful situation:

In the process of trying to make your library media program more flexible and meaningful you have been encouraging teachers to let individual students and small groups make use of library media resources as needed instead of routinely bringing the whole class to the library media center each week. One teacher declares that she will never make this change and says she'll stop having her students use the library media center altogether. You have pointed out the advantages of your being able to work with small groups of the gifted, with slow learners or those who are deficient in particular skills, as well as the value of the extra help you can give to individual students when the entire class doesn't always come at one time. The teacher, however, remains adamant: either the whole class will use the library media center at one time, or they will not come at all. You are dismayed and distressed.

Instead of stewing, you decide to relieve the stress by making a plan for constructive action. You consider possible alternatives: report the situation to the principal or ask the district instructional consultant to talk to the teacher. You discard both of these because the consequences of either would be negative. Either course of action would alienate the teacher and cause further deterioration of relations with her. You decide to handle the situation yourself by taking direct action. In your plan you list in priority order the tasks which must be accomplished:

1. Try to find out why the teacher is being so emotional and stubborn about this. Talk to one of her friends. Maybe she has family problems or doesn't feel well. Perhaps she feels threatened by some other situation in school that you don't know about.
2. Approach her in a conciliatory manner, perhaps over a cup of coffee, or afternoon tea and cookies.
3. Meet her more than halfway and be receptive to her feelings and ideas about her reasons for refusing to consider your proposals.
4. Invite her to observe another teacher's students using the library media center in a flexible manner.
5. Arrange with the principal for another teacher to describe in faculty meeting the results of her use of the library media center for individual students working independently and in small groups.
6. Set up a workshop for all faculty members on flexible uses of the school library media center.
7. Gather relevant material describing flexible use

of the library media center for the development of individual and group projects, and distribute it to all faculty members.
8. See if you can persuade the teacher in question to let some of her students make a more flexible use of the school library media center on a trial basis, while maintaining whole class visits.

Next, list some of the skills you will need to implement your plan. These would include skill in establishing rapport, in creative and empathetic communication, in leadership and in workshop development. Tact and your own integrity and obvious commitment to the best interests of students and teachers will take you a long way toward the possibility of persuading others to conquer their fears and raise their sights by trying something different.

Ask your staff in the library media center for suggestions about your plan and let them share in implementing it. Also keep the principal informed.

Of course, even the best-laid plans don't always meet with success, but you will find that just by trying to do something constructive about the situation that is troubling you, you will have decreased your stress and you will feel more in control. Other suggestions for handling stress were included in a bulletin from the National Institute of Mental Health, reprinted by them, as we are reprinting it here, with permission from the original publisher.

> Recognizing that stress has a lifelong influence on you, what can you do about handling it? Doctors have come up with a few suggestions on how to live with stress.
> 1. Work off stress—If you are angry or upset, try to blow off steam physically by activities such as running, playing tennis, or gardening. Even taking a walk can help. Physical activity allows you a "fight" outlet for mental stress.
> 2. Talk out your worries—It helps to share worries with someone you trust and respect. This may be a friend, family member, clergyman, teacher, or counselor. Sometimes another person can help you see a new side to your problem and thus, a new solution.

If you find yourself becoming preoccupied with emotional problems, it might be wise to seek a professional listener, like a guidance counselor or psychologist. This is not admitting defeat. It is admitting you are an intelligent human being who knows when to ask for assistance.

3. Learn to accept what you cannot change—If the problem is beyond your control at this time, try your best to accept it until you can change it. It beats spinning your wheels, and getting nowhere.

4. Avoid self-medication—Although there are many chemicals, including alcohol, that can mask stress symptoms, they do not help you adjust to the stress itself. Many are habit-forming, so the decision to use them should belong to your doctor. It is a form of flight reaction that can cause more stress than it solves. The ability to handle stress comes from within you, not from the outside.

5. Get enough sleep and rest—Lack of sleep can lessen your ability to deal with stress by making you more irritable. Most people need at least seven to eight hours of sleep out of every 24. If stress repeatedly prevents you from sleeping, you should inform your doctor.

6. Balance work and recreation—"All work and no play can make Jack a nervous wreck." Schedule time for recreation to relax your mind. Although inactivity can cause boredom, a little loafing can ease stress. This should not be a constant escape, but occasionally, you deserve a break.

7. Do something for others—Sometimes when you are distressed, you concentrate too much on yourself and your situation. When this happens, it is often wise to do something for someone else, and get your mind off of yourself. There is an extra bonus in this technique—it helps make friends.

8. Take one thing at a time—It is defeating to tackle all your tasks at once. Instead, set some aside and work on the most urgent.

9. Give in once in awhile—If you find the source of your stress is other people, try giving in instead of

fighting and insisting you are always right. You may find that others will begin to give in, too.

10. Make yourself available—When you are bored and feel left out, go where the action is! Sitting alone will just make you more frustrated. Instead of withdrawing and feeling sorry for yourself, get involved. Is there a play or musical coming up? Chances are they will need help back stage. Get yourself back there and somebody will probably hand you a hammer or paint brush.

From *Current Health*, April 1977 ©1977 by Curriculum Innovations, Inc. Reprinted by permission. Further reproduction prohibited.

Many school systems now are developing system-wide prevention and therapeutic measures against stress in their personnel. An article on "librarian burnout" in *Library Journal* emphasized the effectiveness of Teacher Centers, many of which have been in operation for a decade or more. Teacher Centers, which receive major funding from PL 94-482 legislation, have been, according to Rudolph Bold, the public librarian author, "an unqualified success in positively dealing with the effects of job stress.... A successful example ... is the work done by Dennis Sparks in the Northwest Staff Development Center in Livonia, Michigan.... He uses group therapy techniques to re-involve troubled teachers. A nice touch is that teachers assigned to the center often don't know whether they are being assigned to the center to help or be helped. Frequently it turns out to be both." There are sixty-one centers in existence, and twenty-nine more planned for the future. Still speaking of the Michigan center, Bold says, "... the center's program adds the reinforcement of the group situation in defining the problem, including brainstorming sessions to explore for possible solutions. The final outcome is a contract with oneself to take positive, dated steps toward correction(20)." The point of Bold's description is that such a system would be eminently usable by public libraries as well as school personnel.

In his description of another such Teacher Center, Bold underlines the importance of the professional/personal nature of the cause of stress and its cure or betterment. He characterizes the Bay Shore Teacher Center as being "in-house, yet extrainstitutional." "The 'Center' in this case is located in rooms in various school buildings in the district, usually near the staff cafeteria or teacher's lounge. These centers start their operation an hour or more before the school day begins with rap sessions or interview appointments involving teachers with problems such as increased or inequitable workloads or unjustified exam proctoring assignments. During the day, teachers can spend free periods conferring with colleagues of Fibkins [a clinical psychologist], and lunchtime seminars are available ranging from expert lectures on the runaway problem to informal discussions with a foreign student on his or her impressions of American education. Professional materials such as books and magazines are also freely available at the center."

School library media specialists situated in a school system with access to such a program would be well advised to take advantage of it, or, lacking one, to start a move to replicate it in their own schools.

3
Employer-Sponsored Stress-Reduction Programs

Most of the strategies for coping with stress which have been discussed thus far are self-directed. There have not been many planned programs sponsored by the library professional organizations nor programs designed expressly to meet the many stress-causing factors to which the librarian is subject. A librarian or library media specialist who is experiencing stress has to depend upon personal and individual efforts for relief or seek the services of a local mental health professional or community center. Some relevant programs have been offered at annual library conferences. Also, some library schools have scheduled one- or two-day workshops on techniques for dealing with stress. Some community libraries, responding to a particular user need, will make this subject and methods for alleviation of stress the focal point of a program or presentation, probably learning to meet their own needs in the process. One local library, conscious of the effects of stress upon certain members of the community, sponsored a series of seminars on stress for an especially hard-pressed group: the wives of a large group of unemployed men in the community.

There are two generally recognized types of activities concerned with stress(96). One is called stress education, and it includes seminars, group discussions or short workshops. These sessions serve to raise the consciousness of participants as to symptoms, causes and consequences of stress, and to alert them to helpful coping techniques. Such programs are frequently directed by lay people.

The other area of stress-related activity is called stress management. This is an in-depth approach to stress. In addition to an investigation of causes, the physical conditions and life-styles of participants are appraised, and a step-by-step plan to relieve stress is planned. This program may require a period of six to eight weeks or longer and is directed by a professional, a psychologist, psychiatrist or mental health specialist. It is, in effect, a form of therapy.

The American Institute of Stress, as of 1982, knew of about a hundred and twenty business concerns who were offering either stress education or stress management programs(60). Some companies offer other types of programs which relieve or prevent stress, such as leadership training, physical fitness and the like.

There is a thriving industry devoted to organizing and running stress-related programs, sometimes at rates as high as $2,700 per person. These programs include a variety of techniques: isolation tubs, meditation, exercise, galvanic skin response, self-awareness training, biofeedback, relaxation training, hypnosis, dietary evaluation, psychotherapy and others. It is difficult for employers to select the program which is best for their employees. Mancuso gives some guidelines in selecting stress management programs.(96) In evaluating programs, employers should ask themselves if they include:

goal setting	psychology of stress
conflict management	assertiveness training
time management	biofeedback and/or a system of meditation
delegation	some individualized treatment
information about life stages and crises	information regarding diet and nutrition
behavior techniques for change	health incentive system
role playing with feedback	personality awareness through self-assessment measures

After a program has been selected by an employer, it is essential to see to it that it is properly supervised while being utilized. Guenther charges that all programs are not run well(60).

It is only within the past six to eight years that organizations in industry and public service have turned their attention to the prevalence of stress among their employees. Many companies introduced stress management for economic and political reasons and not just in pure altruistic concern for employees(67). It is said that for every dollar invested in such programs, companies gain a return of five dollars and fifty-two cents in reduced employee absenteeism, increased productivity, and reduced health-insurance costs due to less illness(96). Also, since business has acquired a deteriorating public image, companies wanted to demonstrate that they are concerned about the health and welfare of employees.

It is possible that in future years our professional library organizations—local, regional or national—will become more cognizant of the value of sponsoring programs of stress management, and/or that the agencies that employ them will see fit to undertake this. Our profession could profit from the experiences of those industrial organizations which have developed programs to help their employees cope with stress—to their own as well as their employees' advantage. Let's look at two large companies and their programs.

A. T. & T., faced recently with an extensive reorganization that is changing job titles, duties and whole methods of working for about two hundred and fifty thousand employees, found that "the reorganization was tipping the scales from normal amounts of stress to truly deleterious anxiety reactions"(26). A dozen of its subsidiary Bell companies reacted to the change by strengthening existing programs to help employees cope with change, or initiating new ones. The assistant vice-president for personal relations for Bell Telephone Company of Pennsylvania asked the director for the study of adult development, affiliated with the University of Pennsylvania, to develop a program to meet Bell's needs. The program was tried out with two pilot groups, and adopted company-wide. The cost to the company of the program for twenty-five groups, each composed of twenty managers, was $166,000.

The program began with presentation and discussions on changes in people's lives, including changes in marital and family relations, and how they react to them. Then, the focus was on changes within the company. Next, each participant measured on a graph his or her level of personal achievement, and evaluated relations with others. This was called a "life chart." This was followed by discussion in groups of three participants, called triads, of the life charts of each of the three. The goal of this activity was to show that the problems of individuals are not unique, and that they are not alone in experiencing and coping with them.

This program was considered successful. One district superintendent noted that, at its conclusion, "people are much more open to each other, much more willing to discuss your problems, their problems"(26). Suggestions were made (and by now may have been carried out) to extend the program to lower-level managers and to incorporate some of the principles into management-training seminars.

Even after the reorganization is completed and operating smoothly, "Bell's stress experts believe that the company's newfound desire to deal with employee stress will not diminish, since new sources of stress are bound to develop in the future."

Another large company, Equitable Life Assurance Society of the United States, recognized that during this time of recession there is considerable fear of job loss which causes stress problems.

Some employees become "stress carriers" and infect everyone with whom they come in contact. Equitable offers a full emotional health program for employees, with a staff of four responsible for working with troubled employees in the areas of detection, prevention, education, treatment, referral and follow-up. This service is free of charge to employees and on company time(96).

For those who have lost their jobs, help is given in writing résumés, developing interviews and understanding the policy relating to the termination of positions. These former employees are given three months' pay with released time so that they can investigate other work openings. When possible, they are transferred within the company. Individual and group meetings are held to help them overcome feelings of diminished self-worth (which invariably accompany job termination for whatever cause) and uncertainty about their capabilities, and to face the future.

For those who fear loss of jobs, individual and group meetings are also scheduled. For individuals, stress management can include biofeedback methodology. Equitable has the first biofeedback lab in industry. The treatment phase of five weeks focuses on deep relaxation training and behavior modification for two or three sessions a week. Follow-up consists of evaluations at the end of two weeks, six months and annually.

Other companies are providing stress education or stress management in varying degrees depending upon their resources. Although many companies ignore stress symptoms or simply fire or transfer a troubled employee to a position in which productivity will not be retarded by the employee's problems, others are doing something to help. They may employ counselors to help managers and executives who make problems known. However, some executives do not believe that stress is a problem, or at least one that they want to do anything about. In a 1982 series of interviews with random samplings of executives of the largest concerns, the chief executives of medium-sized companies and proprietors of small businesses, the smallest percentage of those rating stress as a major problem or even somewhat of a problem for them was in the large business group. The largest percentage of those who felt stress was a problem for them was in the small business group(150). One executive of a large corporation explained why he did not have a stress problem: by the time he had arrived at a high position in a large business, he was tough and impervious to stress. Asked how they fended off stress, some executives stated that they don't worry about things, develop interests outside of the business, keep in good physical condition and make sure that they are in the best possible job for them.

Regardless of these opinions, however, some companies even have clinical psychologists to help executives who are experiencing burnout. Treatment is practical, short-term, and goal oriented.

In-house experts provide employee stress-reduction programs or psychological counseling in many companies. Also, educational organizations such as school systems usually have employees on their staffs who have the necessary expertise to conduct such programs (and we mentioned in the previous chapter the growth of teacher burnout prevention and treatment centers). Hospitals are another type of organization which has professional resource people on staff who can conduct stress-relief programs for personnel, and they have long been alert to the stress often caused by the life-and-death crises of hospital life.

Other companies are concentrating on improving the quality of their employees' work-life by means of a wide variety of programs. Some have commissioned organizational climate studies of their operations. Bateman urges managers to alter the characteristics of the work environment. "More often than many employees realize it, it is an active rather than a resigned submissive posture toward stressful circumstances which ultimately provides the most effective coping strategies"(15).

Some companies have not gone beyond the health and exercise or prevention stage in combating stress in their personnel. Large companies such as Xerox and Kimberly Clark have elaborate exercise centers, all types of exercise equipment and health specialists on staff who conduct a comprehensive program of health evaluation, counseling and training exercises. They keep detailed records of health and medical histories. Northern Natural Gas Company has an aerobic program and a fitness center. Bankers Life and Casualty Company of Chicago maintains an after-hours fitness program at the community center across the street from the company offices. Other firms contract with the local YMCA or other existing facility for fitness programs for their employees. Some grant time off from work for exercise and health maintenance.

Higgins and Philips maintain that fitness programs should incorporate adequate recreational activities and include special stress-management aspects such as meditation, biofeedback technique and the like. Eventually successful programs should be extended to workers' families(67).

Those who have had little experience in developing a stress-management plan would probably welcome Weigel and Pinsky's model, which includes the following five steps(155):

1. *Identifying sources of stress*
This is done by using a checklist and by group sharing. Each employee checks those work conditions which are stressful. In group sharing participants identify other sources and discuss them.

2. *Selecting a target*
Employees decide on a target problem with the goal of managing it. For one week they record what happens when the problem occurs. What triggered it? What were they thinking and doing? How did they respond? This record is extremely important in a behavior change program.

3. *Looking for barriers—planning to succeed*
Participants must change negative habits or thinking into a positive commitment to manage stress. Talk about the myth of the perfect manager, the perfect supervisor, the perfect employee. Show how trying to live up to those myths negatively affects job performance. Help them develop a more realistic and acceptable understanding of themselves in relation to the job.

4. *Developing a stress management plan*
Include the following:

> *Self acceptance*
> > Goal setting
> > Value clarification
> > Cognitive restructure
> > Friendship
> > Attitude building
>
> *Skill building*
> > Communication
> > Problem solving
> > Assertiveness
> > Time management
> > Public speaking

Health improvement
  Exercise
  Relaxation
  Weight control
  Recreation/hobbies
  Chemical dependency reduction

Have each participant write a self-contract listing short-term objectives and long-term goals. Specify the specific actions to be practiced for a two-week period. The employee will probably need help in writing this.

5. *Evaluate the plan*
Assess progress made on reaching objectives and goals listed in the self-contract. Establish new ones if necessary.

As library administrators and professional organizations become more sensitive to the needs of personnel, more stress-management programs will be offered at the building or district levels or at the state, regional or national levels. Perhaps before long library personnel will find that it is as crucial for them to learn, either in their academic or in-service training, how to cope with stress as it is to learn the fine points of human relations or how to operate computers.

4
INTERPERSONAL RELATIONS

The library media specialist is at the center of an interpersonal relations web as well as an information network. This might be diagramed as:

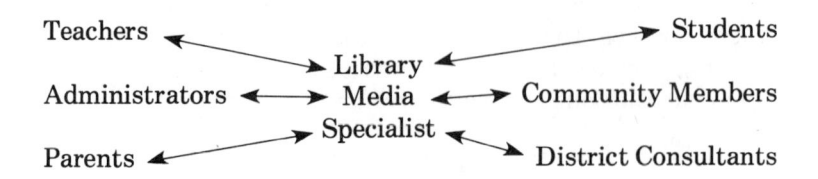

```
Teachers ◄─────────────────────► Students
               ► Library ◄
Administrators ◄────► Media ◄────► Community Members
               ► Specialist ◄
Parents ◄──────                  ► District Consultants
```

Because of this interaction with members of all these groups in the school community, the atmosphere and morale of the whole school may be adversely or favorably affected by the attitudes and behavior of the school library media specialist. One misunderstanding or altercation with a teacher who reports a difficulty to other teachers or parents can poison the working relationships in the school. This type of disruption of relations with an individual in any one of the above groups can cause the library media specialist to experience stress. On the other hand, the maintenance of good relations can help create a comfortable, pleasant working environment.

Since you occupy such a central position in your school, you will want to make each connecting strand a positive force for good relations. In order to do this, it is first necessary to develop your own self-esteem. Your self-image must be strong enough and positive enough so that you can be sensitive to the needs and feelings of others without being unduly vulnerable to thoughtless, or even malicious, remarks and actions by some.

Second, you must have good communication skills, both verbal and nonverbal. Verbal communications must be clear, concise and easily understood by the receiver. Nonverbal communication includes eye contact, facial expression, body posture, hand and body movements, tone of voice and manner of dress. Martin also calls attention to the errors often made in communication(97):

> Not organizing thoughts well before speaking.
> Including too many ideas and making comprehension difficult.
> Not realizing that the receiver of the message may be influenced in his or her understanding by intrinsic factors such as needs, opinions, attitudes, beliefs or expectations.
> As a receiver of messages, letting attention wander or be distracted by nearby activities. (This is very apt to happen if the communication takes place in the library media center.)
> Indicating as receiver that we have understood the message by making statements which evaluate, judge or disapprove, and so chill the communication process.

Added to these frequently made errors is the fact that the sender and receiver of messages may often have different backgrounds and past experiences and therefore perceive situations and ideas differently. Communication is seldom a perfect process and we should take this into consideration when we seek to transmit information to others.

Verbal and nonverbal messages should reinforce each other, and be "in sync." The library media specialist is not very convincing in telling a teacher "That's fine!" while tightening the lips around clenched teeth!

Communication can be improved by finding ways to generate feedback from the receiver so that you can assess whether or not the message was received accurately, and judge the reaction.

In addition to good communication you will want to give attention to other interpersonal skills. Johnson describes four areas in which to develop capabilities(74):

1. Knowing and trusting each other. This requires self-awareness and self-acceptance, being aware of your strengths and capabilities, and being able to disclose your thoughts, feelings and beliefs to others.
2. Accurately and unambiguously understanding each other. Establishing your self-worth will enable you to reach out and understand others better. The communication process described above facilitates this process.
3. Influencing and helping each other. This reaches to the heart of library media services. You establish a reputation for expertly and cheerfully working with teachers, students and others in the school community to upgrade learning options and progress. You build the self-esteem of others which indicates that you value their worth.
4. Constructively resolving problems and conflicts. This was addressed in the previous chapter, and it is vital to maintaining good relationships.

All of this is possible while at the same time maintaining an impersonal friendliness suitable to professional relationships. It is essential for you to avoid being drawn into criticism or gossip about others and taking words or actions personally. Beware of faculty cliques, and of taking sides in any "us versus them" controversy.

Some other suggestions for improving interpersonal relations would include the following:

You will want to try to be especially helpful to someone who has been uncooperative, since your goal is to develop an excellent library media program that will successfully serve everyone in your school population.

If your temper has a short fuse, dampen it. Always use reasonable discussion rather than hot words to resolve a conflict.

Make yourself as accessible as possible to teachers, students, administrators and parents. Find ways to work with them on student learning activities and to bring people and materials together in new and exciting ways.

Be alert, welcoming and equitable in your dealings with everyone. Students prize the quality of "fairness" above almost all others. Playing favorites, or seeming to do so, invites dissension.

Maintain your credibility as a knowledgeable faculty member and media specialist in all types of resources of information.

Become a learning model by following a regular program of reading and study to enhance and update your expertise.

Be open-minded and tolerant of the ideas and plans of others. A judgmental attitude blocks inspiration and creativity.

Good interpersonal relationships are so vital to your work that any effort you expend in improving them is returned tenfold in the quality of your library media program and in a prevailing tension-free atmosphere.

5
Relations with Administrators

The cooperation and support of the school principal resulting from a sound relationship between you and that administrator is a must for your mental health and for the success of your work. Conflict with the principal or other administrator is a constantly recurring flashpoint for stress. This stress is exacerbated because administrators are authority figures and you may feel that your job security is threatened.

Before you accept a position you will have a conference with the principal of the school for which you are being hired. At that conference you should assess as exactly as possible what the principal's philosophy of education is, and what expectations it carries for your role and for the library media program as a whole. If the principal seems committed to a textbook-centered type of learning, traditional instructional methods only and a rigid schedule for use of the library media center, and if you do not want to run the kind of program such a philosophy imposes, you had better pass up that position.

The trouble is, of course, that school library media jobs are not plentiful these days, and many who are searching for a position are tempted to take whatever is offered and try later to make the necessary adjustments. However, if you are committed to directing a library media program made excellent by its full integration with the instructional program, your differences with the principal will undoubtedly lead to conflict and stress.

The following is a simulated conference between a principal and a library media specialist who is being interviewed for a vacancy in the library media center:

> PRINCIPAL: I've reviewed your personal and professional qualifications and find that they are acceptable. I can offer you the position.
>
> LIBRARY MEDIA SPECIALIST: I'd like you to tell me something about your educational philosophy, your school and your expectations for the library media program.
>
> PRINCIPAL: My philosophy is to make students learn up to the standard of their grade level or to retain them for a year in the same grade. My main concern is discipline. I expect each teacher to schedule his or her class to the library once a week. This will provide the teacher with an opportunity to grade papers, plan work and prepare reports. Since teachers rely on textbooks for their instruction I expect students will use the library mainly for recreational reading. Your role is to keep the books in order, circulate them and keep the library quiet.
>
> LIBRARY MEDIA SPECIALIST: I believe in broadening and deepening the scope of instruction by encouraging the use of many different print and nonprint materials. I see my role as including planning of instructional units with teachers and facilitating creative teaching methods. I have always worked with many individual students and small groups in the library media center to meet their special needs and promote independent learning. I would want the library media program to become fused with the instructional program. I would encourage students to use nonprint materials together with printed ones as learning resources, and I would teach them how to produce their own unique materials. Discipline would not be my chief emphasis in the media center, and would not need to be because I would concentrate on helping students find and use the resources they need to be productively occupied. I would want to make the

library media center an attractive, pleasant place that students enjoy coming to.

This applicant is obviously not the one for this position. There is great potential for stress inherent in such divergent philosophies.

Here is another principal/library media specialist interview:

> PRINCIPAL: From my review of your qualifications I believe you could help upgrade my library. I know that the role of the librarian has changed recently but I need more information. I believe in promoting a pleasant learning environment and having eager, motivated students. I believe we should use whatever means and materials are necessary to help each student reach his or her own potential. My management of the school is firm but understanding. I would hope that an expanded library program will be compatible with my philosophy. How do you define your role?
>
> LIBRARY MEDIA SPECIALIST: I see my role as moving the library media specialist into partnership with teachers to develop stimulating learning opportunities based on the use of a wide variety of print and nonprint resources. I would like to participate in the periodic revising of the curriculum and in devising innovative instructional methods. I would increase communication with teachers and keep them informed not only about the library media center's own holdings but resources from outside the building as well. I would acquaint teachers and students with the operation and use of technologies such as video and computers. I would like to confer with you frequently about the media program. Would the kind of program I have described be consistent with your school management philosophy? How does it compare with your expectations of my role? Also, I would like to have a better understanding of your responsibilities for the operation of the total school program.

Although these two might not agree on everything there is a good chance that they will have a fine relationship and will work well together.

Casciano-Savignano lists the impediments to an effective relationship between faculty members and the principal(28):

Inconsistent policies
Non-support of decisions made by faculty members, especially when parents are involved.
Non-availability
Lack of communication
Unapproachability
Authoritarianism
Lack of support in discipline problems
Disregard of the opinions and suggestions of faculty members
Partiality
Lack of appreciation of faculty efforts

You will find that one of the most useful tools to develop rapport with the principal is the regularly scheduled conference. One of your chief aims during early discussions is to be certain that the principal really understands the features of an excellent library media program, the role you hope to play in the total school program, and the various ways you and the classroom teachers can collaborate in designing a stronger instructional program. Respect begets respect, and as you talk with the principal you will want to show your respect for his or her professional competence and for any ideas and suggestions offered. You will receive information about the principal's responsibilities for total school administration, and shape within them your joint expectations for your role in this larger framework. In your future conferences you should be able to expect consultation, guidance and helpful suggestions about many of the following(98):

The principal expects the library media staff to:
Be responsible for the development of immediate and long-range goals and objectives.
Demonstrate a philosophy of pleasant, enthusiastic service to all students and teachers.
Recognize that the major portion of your time should be devoted to active involvement with pupils and teachers.
Serve in the capacity of media expert.

Administer the media center so as to provide flexible accessibility.
Schedule materials selection and curriculum planing conferences with teachers.
Plan and develop with teachers a comprehensive program of instruction in the use of materials.
Maintain an attractive, comfortable library media center with inviting atmosphere.
Develop the library media center as a true multimedia resource.
Pursue a program of keeping informed about new educational practices and new materials and educational equipment.
Develop a balanced materials collection which reflects the curriculum, teacher interests and student interests and needs.
Exhibit leadership in developing a school materials selection policy.
Publicize the services of the media staff and the materials in the library media center.
Cooperate in planning developmental reading programs.
Assist teachers and students in the production of instructional materials.
Evaluate media services periodically.
Serve on curriculum and planning committees.
Provide an excellent organization of materials and equipment of all types so that they are easily accessible.
Offer services outside the walls of the media center by scheduling visits to classes and other group meetings.
Provide materials and services for students with varying ability levels and learning styles.
Develop with a faculty-student committee a flexible set of library media center rules and regulations.
Submit frequent reports to the principal on pertinent library media center facts, figures and activities.
Become knowledgeable about new technologies and

assume a leadership role in helping teachers and students use them effectively.

Participate in publicizing the library media program and the school program in the community.

Originate research projects or assist in ongoing research in the school.

Discussions held during conferences with the principal will interpret and clarify many of these expectations. You will report on your progress in achieving them and ask for the principal's assistance and support when needed.

It is important to emphasize that these are not "your goals" for "your program," but rather goals in support of the instructional program which you and the library media center have an important role in implementing. Much can be accomplished when the principal really sees this, and the principal and the library media specialist can work in harmony toward goals they see as common goals. Their good rapport is the firm rock upon which an excellent and effective library media program, as one facet of an overall exemplary school program, is built. (See Appendix B for further material on principal/library media specialist relationships.)

EXAMPLE OF A STRESS-CREATING SITUATION

In this elementary school all faculty members are required to assume some non-instructional duties. The principal has assigned you to before- and after-school bus duty. You believe that the library media center should be open for service at these times. Since you don't have a media aide you will have to close the center to attend to bus duty. You want to accept your share of non-instructional duties, but those that you have been assigned will be injurious to the library media program and limit access for the students and teachers.

STRESS-REDUCTION RESPONSE

After considering any side effects, which of the following would you choose as the most effective alternative?

1. You keep your resentment bottled up and carry out your bus duty.

2. You schedule a conference with the principal and explain the need to keep the library media center open before and after school. You remind the principal that state and regional standards require this.
3. You know a friend of the state director of elementary education and you ask your friend to report the situation.
4. You ask the principal to let you swap duties with another teacher and, after much effort, you arrange to substitute taking up tickets at basketball and football games for the bus duty.
5. You ask the principal for a monthly conference to discuss the features of an excellent library media program, and ask advice about various aspects of the program.

(You may want to know that this actually happened, and that the alternative #4 worked best.)

6
Relations with Teachers

Teachers and library media specialists working at cross purposes are frequently the cause of tension and stress. A library media specialist may operate under inflexible policies, and have poor communication and lack participation in curriculum development; the teachers may lack understanding of the library media program and the role of the media specialist, and harbor resentment of the perceived "soft job" of the media specialist. All this can provide the dry tinder for a conflagration in interpersonal relations.

As we have said, one of your professional duties is to maintain good relations with teachers. Since the success of your program depends largely upon this, the impetus for improving relations should come from you.

Here, again, how you feel about yourself is paramount. You must try to perceive yourself in positive ways, as being liked and accepted. If you feel confident of your competencies and abilities to work well with others it is easier for you to reach out, and you will be secure enough to risk possible rejection. Johnson states, "If you think well of yourself you are likely to think well of others.... A self-rejecting person expects to be rejected by others and will tend to reject them"(74).

Some remarks that teachers might make could lead to poor relations:

"You can't ever find what you want in the library."
"There's not enough material on my subject."
"There's too much noise in the library."
"The librarian is so careful to keep everything in exact order that I'm afraid to touch any materials."
"The librarian never has time to help me."
"I can't check out materials for as long as I want them."
"The librarian is always sending my students back to my classroom."
"The librarian just has a few students in the library while I have thirty-five or forty each period."

On the other hand, there are some remarks the library media specialist might make that set the stage for poor relations:

"Teachers don't know the value of the multi-media approach."
"They don't know which materials are available in the library media center."
"They don't know how to use equipment."
"They can't make suggestions for additional materials for the subjects they teach."
"They don't believe I know enough to help improve instruction."
"They don't believe I really want to help them."
"They don't know how to plan for productive student use of the library media center."
"They don't support my policy of student behavior in the library media center."

Let it be emphasized that these remarks do not reflect the attitudes of most teachers and library media specialists. They are quoted merely to show where points of friction and resentment may arise unless the library media specialist is diligent in pursuing strategies to build pleasant, understanding relationships. Reading them through should point up two "don'ts": don't generalize ("they" are all individuals and like to be thought of that way), and don't criticize. As we all learned long ago, but sometimes forget, "If you can't say something nice, don't say anything."

To achieve the good relationships you need, you might want to follow some of the suggestions below.

On a personal level:
Show teachers that you respect them and their knowlege of their disciplines.
Show that you consider and esteem each teacher as an individual.
Try to keep attuned to teachers' personal needs for information, and suggest materials that might be helpful.
Disregard gossip and discourage it.
Promote informal get-togethers.
Let teachers know that you enjoy working with them and that your door is always open.

It would be a good idea to ask teachers to complete a short informal questionnaire to help you know them better. Include such questions as: What types of fiction and nonfiction do you enjoy? Are you a craftsman? May we exhibit your work? What leisure activities do you pursue?

And on a professional level:
Try, over time, to reach a consensus on educational philosophy with each teacher.
Devise opportunities for teachers to share learning opportunities with others.
Take time to communicate frequently and stay alert to problems teachers may be having in relation to the year's or semester's work so that you can offer assistance.
Exhibit awareness and interest in areas that many teachers find especially difficult, such as the preparation for and management of student search projects and papers. You can do much to help them improve student opportunities and teachers' workflow.
Remember that it is up to you to ensure that teachers have an up-to-date understanding of our role and its potential for supporting their work and that of the students.
Involve teachers and students in setting policies

for use of library media resources and be certain that all understand them.

Involve teachers in formulating the objectives for the library media program and helping to implement them. Set priorities with them, not for them.

Discuss student needs and interests with teachers.

Talk with teachers about the various ways they may make use of the library media resources and your services, and plan activities cooperatively with them. Help them devise creative teaching strategies.

Schedule a planning session with each teacher periodically, but at least once a month, to assist in planning instructional units, learning packages or learning centers.

Offer to secure materials from sources outside the school. Make clear to teachers that the library media center is an entry point to a vast network of resources.

Plan instruction in library skills jointly with teachers in terms of need for those skills arising from the curriculum, and visit the classroom with materials specific to the needs.

Be sure that teachers as well as students understand library procedures and processes and, especially, that they feel comfortable with all reference tools, and all forms of media and equipment.

Keep teachers well informed about items in the professional collection and solicit suggestions for additions that they would find useful.

Publicize the work of teachers—and their students—who make especially creative and effective use of the library media center's materials, equipment and services.

Finally, you yourself can:

Keep well informed about the latest development in the library media field (including such new media as computers and video forms), in curriculum development and in instructional methods.

Administer the library media center so that it is as fully accessible as possible and so the materials are arranged for consultation with ease and convenience.

Attend departmental meetings and curriculum revision committee meetings.

Be well informed, and show it, about the total school program: sports, plays, clubs—who won and what's new.

Be receptive to requests by teachers, and willing to change procedures when this will promote the use of materials.

A pleasant, cooperative relationship between teachers and the library media specialist can work wonders in the total school program and can restrain the emergence of stressful situations.

Stress-Creating Situation

In this middle school your relations with one teacher, Mrs. Rogers, have greatly deteriorated. The school owns only one video-tape recorder. Mrs. Rogers borrowed it from the library media center and, though you have requested it several times, has not returned it. Mrs. Rogers is considered an excellent teacher and has made exceptionally effective use of the library media center. You don't want to disrupt her plans but other teachers are waiting to use the VTR and are complaining to you.

Stress-Reduction Response

After considering any side effects, which of the following would you choose as the most effective alternative?
1. You evaluate your relations with Mrs. Rogers. Have you been too compliant? too accommodating? Does she respect your professional competence? You've never had any problems gaining the cooperation of other teachers.
2. You go to Mrs. Rogers's classroom when she is not there and bring the VTR back to the library media center.

3. You discuss the situation with a supportive friend and with the district library media consultant and ask their advice.
4. You report Mrs. Rogers's behavior to the school principal.
5. You talk with Mrs. Rogers in a friendly manner and find out how she is using the VTR. You tell her in a firm but pleasant way that she must share the VTR with the other teachers, and that as soon as she has finished her current project with the equipment you will send for it, but no later than the end of the week.

7
RELATIONS WITH STUDENTS

Breathes there the librarian with soul so dead that never to him or herself has said, "These kids are driving me crazy!" You will often find your patience exhausted, your efforts unavailing and your interpersonal relations fractured by students who consistently are doing no reading or work in the library media center. Instead, they are worrying others, cruising the area talking to friends, mishandling equipment and causing a disturbance using the microcomputer or playing rock records in the conference room. These are only a few of the problems with those students who apparently have no motivation to learn.

To reduce the stress caused by student misbehavior you need to develop an action plan to use as you work with such students. However, first you need to know more about them, their needs, fears, desires, goals. (See Appendix C for chart of child's needs.)

Psychologists tell us about the developmental stages of children and young people. Your understanding of this will affect your reaction to them. Some features of these stages are:

Early primary children: Adjustment to separation from mother; need to establish close, warm relationships with substitute adult figures; need to develop trust in adults; need help in controlling impulses and behavior; need encouragement in verbalizing their anxieties, loneliness, pleasures, successes.

Pre- and early adolescence: Anxiety and mild behavior disturbances; need a continuing, warm relationship with someone they can trust and believe is interested in them.

Early adolescence: Increase in anxiety and tension due to control of sexual impulses, physical growth, body changes, independence and future life roles.

Adolescence: The above tensions are increased and, in addition, the struggle to be accepted by their peers and to prepare for a vocation causes extra pressures.

Another factor to keep in mind is the background of some of these students. They may have experienced insecurity, rejection, delinquency, drug addiction, family tensions, violence, street crime and many self-identity and learning problems. On the other hand, some of the students with the worst behavior problems come from comfortable, middle-class environments. But while many have had an abundance of material things, they have not experienced caring family relationships.

You may believe that strict discipline should be your watchword in your relation with these students, and you engage in a continuing battle to enforce rigid, often unrealistic, rules. By loosening up on this punitive attitude you could relieve much stress, letting them know that you value them as persons and find something good in them in spite of their misbehavior. A caring, understanding attitude on your part would go a long way in solving many discipline problems.

For an overt expression of this viewpoint you might include in your plan the following creed for library media personel quoted by Martin and Carson(98):

1. I will spend the majority of my time working with the children and teachers rather than with "things."

2. I will make every child feel welcome in the library, even those who misbehave.

3. I will treat every child with the same courtesy as I would an adult.
4. I will gear my instruction to the individual ability level of students.
5. I will take time to talk with students about their interests and concerns.
6. I will learn as many students' names as possible and call them often by name.
7. I will remember to show students that I care about them.
8. I will try to find something to praise about children who have behavior problems.
9. I will remember that I communicate as much with my body as I do with my oral expression.
10. I will make the library media center as attractive and as inviting as possible.
11. I will take time to look at children when they want to talk to me.
12. I will let children see that I have a sense of humor.
13. I will find many opportunities to reinforce students' acceptable behavior instead of always reprimanding students who are misbehaving.
14. I will evaluate the rules and regulations governing the use of media and will eliminate those which inhibit access to use.
15. I will enforce the remaining rules firmly but pleasantly.

You might also include in your action plan for working with these students some of the following ideas:

> Work with them as much as possible on an individual or small group basis.
> Plan many activities and projects based on their interests.
> Invite community members with expertise in special areas to come and talk on topics the students choose.
> Increase the collection in your library media center career corner and invite the guidance counselor to talk with these students on the wise choice of

a career.

Work with them individually to increase their interest in ideas, their motivation to learn and their reading and other language skills.

Teach them the techniques of making slide-tape sequences, sets of transparencies, 8mm films, or video-tape programs. The recognition they receive when they present their programs to their classmates raises their self-esteem, and this good feeling is reflected in their behavior.

Provide opportunities for each student to experience success as an individual and to contribute to the success of a group enterprise.

Maintain your goal of helping each student to reach his or her potential.

Arrange attractive bulletin board displays and exhibits to stimulate students' interest in reading and in using materials.

Add an ample collection of paperback books, games and puzzles.

Secure funds for the addition of one or more microcomputers. Work toward one per twenty students.

Make use of nonprint materials, filmstrips and slides, as well as books, to set up learning centers on camping, physical fitness, sports, snakes, scuba diving, space travel, or any interest which arises.

When these students understand that you really care about them and are sincerely interested in their concerns, your relations with them will mend, their behavior will improve and your stress will diminish.

STRESS-CREATING SITUATION

You thought you would scream if you looked up one more time and saw that same student coming into the high school library media center for the third time that day, always with no purpose. He roams around and sometimes sits flipping the pages of a magazine while he talks to friends. You have tried to find some books he'd like to read but he doesn't seem to be interested in anything. You've talked with his teachers and they say that he has plenty of work to do. He has already failed a course and has been assigned to a second period in a study hall.

STRESS-REDUCTION RESPONSE

After considering side effects, which of the following would you choose as the most effective alternative?

1. You try to find something about his interests and needs by consulting his teachers and the permanent record of his progress filed in the school office.
2. You ask his counselor to investigate and if she thinks it advisable to schedule a conference with his teachers and parents which you would attend.
3. You report him to the principal.
4. You give him some jobs to do in the library media center and make opportunities to talk with him in a caring, friendly manner.
5. You work with his social studies teacher to develop a project for him involving a slide-tape production. You teach him the technical skills and supervise his work.
6. You secure some microcomputer programs on reading skills and ask his teachers to monitor his use of them.
7. You collect several paperback books you think he might like on his reading level, which is three grades below his grade level. You schedule a conference with him and let him choose one of the books to read. You tell him you'd like to keep the book in your office for him to read when he comes to the library media center.

8
RELATIONS WITH PARENTS AND COMMUNITY MEMBERS

Another group with whom you will interact and which has the potential of involving you in stressful situations is the group of parents and other people in the community.

Ten or fifteen years ago the participation of members of the public in school affairs was not welcomed. Then it came to be understood that many had skills which were of great value to the school program, and also that family/home reinforcement and support of students is of paramount importance to successful learning. Parents and others were encouraged to volunteer their services in the library media center, health room, and other areas. They were recognized as aides, tutors and resource speakers on topics within their experience. Now parents and other citizens have become active in the school decision-making processes and serve on many advisory committees, such as those concerned with media services, materials selection, curriculum development, and others.

It is imperative for the library media specialist and staff to maintain good relations with these parents and community members to avoid personal stress and to promote desirable public relations. Stress points are:

> The challenges to the appropriateness of materials in the library media center.

Disagreement over the library media specialist's policies in the media center.

Insistence on the part of volunteers that they use their own procedures rather than those of the library media specialist.

Disregard for school regulations.

Before community members start participating in the school program, you might ask the principal about the desirability of drawing up a policy concerning volunteer service in the school if there is not one already in place. The principal might appoint a committee, including parents, to develop the policy. You should be sure that all volunteers have a copy of the policy and are familiar with it before they start to work. Some school districts have such a policy district-wide, sometimes approved by the school board. (See Appendix D for a policy from one school district.)

The stress point that is most prevalent at the present time springs from the attempt by pressure groups to remove books or other materials from the library media center shelves if the content does not happen to coincide with their views. These views are usually either moral, religious or political, and sometimes all three at once. Diverse sets of standards and values are involved, and sometimes the grounds for displeasure may concern the author's political or religious ideas even if the content of a particular book in question raises no objections.

This kind of controversy causes the library media specialist much anxiety. Some try to bypass it by exercising a kind of self-censorship and do not order titles they think may be challenged. Or they may order such titles and restrict their use. Woods and Salvatore state: "In order for library media centers to survive as viable institutions that present all viewpoints, librarians must be more knowledgeable about censorship practices and, moreover, must be prepared to defend their selections"(160).

The best defense against censorship is the school district's materials selection policy.

This policy, approved by the Board of Education, is one that every school district should have. It should contain not only the principles of selection but also the procedure to be followed when materials are challenged, including the process to be followed for re-evaluation of challenged materials. A committee of library media specialists, teachers, parents and possibly students should serve on the re-evaluation committee, and members of these same groups, plus an administrator and/or a representative of the board, should develop the policy in the first place. One problem is that some principals panic when confronted by an angry parent speaking in general terms of "dirty books," and hastily have the offending books removed from the library media center instead of following the procedures in the policy. A cardinal rule is that all complaints must be made in writing, and that references be made specific. (See Appendix E for a sample materials selection policy.)

You need to be familiar with Supreme Court rulings on censorship. A 1982 decision stipulated that the Board of Education of a school district did not have the authority to remove books from their school libraries because they disagreed with the ideas expressed in the books. It is a good idea also for you to be familiar with the various "bills of rights" and freedom-to-read statements that have been issued not only by librarians but by English teachers (NCTE) and other groups over the past thirty years.

Those who have not had the experience do not realize the amount of stress aroused by being faced with parents who are very upset, and sometimes abusive, demanding the removal of books. You can stay in control of the situation if you are able to remain calm and pleasant, explaining the district policy for registering complaints about books and describing your method of selecting books.

If you need help in combating censorship attempts you can contact the Intellectual Freedom Committee of the American Library Association, 50 E. Huron St., Chicago, IL 60611.

You will need to put to use all your interpersonal relations skills and your leadership expertise in dealing with volunteers and with materials challenges.

The functioning of these two policies will do much to avert conflicts and stress. The following are some other ways you can improve relations with parents and community members:

    1. Always exhibit congeniality, good nature and a welcoming attitude toward them.
    2. Demonstrate your appreciation of their contributions.

3. Provide a working environment which is attractive and efficient.

4. Make available a collection of materials specially geared to the interests and needs of parents and others in the community, such as materials on child growth and development, parenting, adolescence, retirement, the care of the physically and mentally disabled, the slow learner, etc. You can secure the permission of the principal to circulate materials to these adults.

5. Publish lists of new books in the PTA newsletter.

6. Publicize your collection and encourage visits to the library media center.

7. In cooperation with school district instructional consultants, develop home teaching packages to circulate.

8. Involve parents in your program for exceptional children.

9. Organize study groups to meet after school or in the evening to discuss topics of interest. Invite school district consultants to attend these meetings to provide guidance and counsel. For instance, a discussion on reading would benefit from the reading consultant's suggestions.

10. Participate in the school's adult education program.

11. Hold classes in computer operation and use, demonstrating with the library media center's microcomputer. Give instructions on how to access local or national data bases.

Before making an all-out effort to serve community members, Barron suggests that the following questions be answered(13):

> Is your school involved in a community education program?
> Is grant money available for such a project?
> Is money available to pay professional and support staff?
> Do district policies permit or deny access to the school system's materials?
> Do you have sufficient resources to share?

Are cooperative ventures with other libraries possible?

Remember that policies which might inhibit such activities between school library media centers and the larger community probably can be changed, and that lack of money can be turned from an obstacle into an opportunity. Already many communities, realizing the importance of strengthening the family/school partnership, have sought funds for parent and community education materials from local business and industry. Joining forces to develop reading motivation and enjoyment is proving particularly successful. Families and schools jointly can involve community groups and such resources as local radio and television stations in in-school and out-of-school learning for both children and adults(7).

At a time when the proportion of citizens with children in school is shrinking rapidly, community involvement in school affairs can be a big plus for the schools. The library media specialist can be particularly effective in demonstrating to the taxpayers the enduring, lifelong values of education and in gaining their support and interest. Structuring a plan to build these good relations with parents and other community members can turn them into learning advocates and library advocates as well, and relieve and even eliminate stressful situations.

STRESS-CREATING SITUATION

Two parents come to your high school library media center and complain that their children are never allowed time to use the media center. These are very bright students and have scheduled classes every period and no study hall. The parents are upset. They have to take the students to the public library to secure the materials they need. The students can't stay after school to use the library media center because they are in car pools and must leave immediately after school. The parents resent the fact that their children can't use the school library media center.

STRESS-REDUCTION RESPONSE

After considering any side effects, which of the following would you choose as the most effective alternative?

1. You show the parents that you understand their concern and suggest that they talk with the principal.
2. You talk with the students' counselor and ask him to set up a conference with the principal, the students' parents and teachers.
3. You talk with the students' social studies and science teachers and suggest that the students be allowed to do an independent study which will not require regular class attendence. You offer to help them identify materials to use and to supervise their work in the library media center.
4. You ask the district instructional consultant's help in encouraging the students' teachers to organize their classes so that individuals can come to the library media center during class time.

9
THE DYNAMICS OF CHANGE

Change is one of the constants in our lives. Children know this but adults don't really want to believe it because they are firmly embedded in their comfortable, familiar, static way of life.

Abrego and Brammer(2) define change or transitions as "those events in which an individual

1. experiences a personal awareness of discontinuity in his/her life space, and
2. must develop new behavioral responses because the situation is new and/or the required behavioral adjustments are novel".

The above authors also state that our attitudes toward change affect the way we interpret events. This initial interpretation determines our style of responding to change. If your attitude is fatalistic, resentful, hopeless, powerless, anxious, you probably will not attempt to respond to change. When these emotions take over, stress symptoms appear—migraine headaches, ulcers and other illnesses. If your attitude is that you have survived other changes and that change presents interesting challenges, then you are likely to feel calmer and more in control, and able to respond to change with clear, realistic reasoning in a constructive way.

You will probably have more than one type of change to respond to. The literature lists two: planned and random. Mandated change might be considered a third type, though it may or may not be planned. Random or chance change is usually so diffuse and impermanent that it probably does not present a problem. Planned change is a structured process guided by a change agent, someone who has vision, initiative, stamina, authority and charisma. This person might be the school principal, the district consultant, the library media specialist or a teacher. Planned change is usually accomplished by the following process or one similar to it:

> Development of a need for change, or generating the recognition of such a need.
> Establishing good communication among all those involved.
> Making provision for those involved to participate in the planning.
> Gathering information about alternate courses of action.
> Evaluating these and selecting the one to be implemented.
> Identifying resources necessary to do the job.
> Implementing a chosen alternative with the commitment of all involved.
> Evaluating effectiveness and revising plans if necessary.

Mandated change is directed from on high, from the superintendent, principal, or state department of education. It may be, for example, a directive that all teachers will emphasize the basics, or develop programs for the gifted, or "mainstream" exceptional children into regular classes, or move to individualize instruction. Sometimes but not always, school personnel are asked to participate in planning these changes, and sometimes training is provided to enable personnel to cope with the changes.

Lippitt warns us about the forces against change(90):

> Fear of failure or awkwardness in trying to initiate a new practice.
> Reluctance to admit weaknesses.

63

Fatalistic expectation of failure because of previous unsuccessful attempts.

Fear of losing some current satisfaction. Members' imperfect awareness of their own interpersonal processes. Ideological resistance to self-appraisal.

School community's lack of mechanism for making decisions.

To these we might add:

Emotional upheavals caused by change.

Failure to accept the inevitability of change and its accelerating rate.

Inadequate training in the use of new instructional methods and materials.

Little or no involvement in planning the processes of change.

Lack of support from the school principal.

Failure of the administration to provide adequate materials and equipment.

A coping strategy for change can prevent tension from being transformed into stress. Antonovsky finds three major variables that enter into every coping strategy(6):

Rationality—the accurate, objective evaluation of extent to which the change is a threat.

Flexibility—the availability of contingency plans and tactics and of a willingness to consider them. Openness to new information.

Farsightedness—anticipation of the response of the environment, internal and external, to the actions envisaged by the strategy.

As you develop a pattern of coping with change you need to remember three key words: *evaluate, select, act. Evaluate* the change situation, *select* an alternative from among several considered, along with their positive and negative aspects, and *act* or put into operation the selected alternative.

Example:
All social studies classes have been required to develop instructional units on global interrelationships.
You assess the change and decide that the threat to you comes from the fact that you are not very knowledgeable about the subject and relevant resources.
You consider alternative courses of action: Withdraw, in effect; keep a low profile and don't get involved. Positive aspect: you won't have the hassle of trying to cope by working on the development of instructional units and trying to find materials for them with teachers. Negative aspect: you'll miss an opportunity for professional growth and your credibility with teachers, students and possibly the principal will suffer. You decide on the other alternative of taking an active part in preparing for the change.
You put this alternative into operation. You meet with various groups and help devise the instructional units. You suggest learning experiences for class groups and individuals. You identify relevant materials in your collection, both print and nonprint. You search recommended lists of materials for items to be purchased. First and foremost, you read all you can find on the subject. You ask the principal to sponsor a series of workshops with a consultant who is an authority on the subject.

Some results of the way you have handled this situation, in addition to the benefits for students, are the growth of your professional skills, the rise in your self-esteem, the boost in your reputation for proficiency and leadership and the reduction of your stress. Also, you have begun the process of developing a strategy of coping with change.

Griffin summarizes our lives today: "Transience permeates our time deeply . . . influences our living patterns, unsettles our business system, saturates our arts, renders obsolete every new technology." But, he concludes, "better the restless search and discords of change than complacency in shopworn forms and sterile ideas"(59).

There seems little doubt that, as we move toward the year 2000 and a new century, the problems to be faced nationwide and worldwide will make themselves felt in some degree in even the most isolated and complacent of communities. In 1980, a wide-ranging report on projected conditions was published under the joint auspices of the U.S. State Department and the President's Council on Environmental Quality, entitled *The Global 2000 Report to the President.* Three years in the making, the report represented findings and analysis from thirteen agencies of the federal government. The picture presented of a more crowded, more highly polluted and more unstable society than we have now demands a course of action and change if solutions are to be found, and the threats to our very existence are to be in any degree turned back. This report reaffirms the findings of others that have been prepared over the past decade or so by knowledgeable groups. The panel is quoted as saying in the report that there are "no quick fixes" and that "the only solutions . . . are complex and longterm because the difficulties are inextricably linked to some of the most perplexing and persistent problems in the world—poverty, injustice and social conflict." The report concludes with the optimistic belief that disaster can be prevented by taking "determined new initiatives" with the United States in a strong leadership role(140).

Though all of this may seem far away from the localized evidences of change that must be dealt with in the school building, the classroom and the library media center, in fact it is not. The instability, the crowding and the resulting stress show up in the daily lives of every one of us. The school library media specialist who is aware of the global sources of the need to change, to begin to find solutions, will perhaps be able to tackle the job confidently, and help colleagues and teachers to do so, too.

10
NEW TECHNOLOGIES

One change which has always been traumatic for teachers and librarians is any change in the media used in instruction. Many, many years ago, when record players, radio, and glass slides were introduced, librarians and teachers were at first uncertain, frustrated and apprehensive about their use. Some made no attempt to consider these new media as instructional tools.

How much more likely is the potential for stress today with the rapid proliferation of changes in the communication and computer technologies. Cornish quotes the Stanford University economist Edward Steinmuller, who in writing about microcomputers states, "If the airlines had progressed as rapidly as this technology the Concorde would be carrying half a million passengers at 20 million miles an hour for less than a penny each"(35).

Another indication of the rate of change is the fact that the first commercially available microcomputer was sold in 1975, and today experts agree that microcomputers will become as much a part of our lives in the near future as the telephone and television. Computer literacy may soon be considered as basic as the three R's. Writing in 1981, Cornish predicted that "microcomputing advances, possible within five years, are mind-boggling"(35). Pogrow believes "the integration of the television with the telephone, computer, and videodisc represents as fundamental an innovation as the development of the printing press"(113). The new technologies in communications and computers, sometimes abbreviated as "compunications," will produce great changes in society, industry, government, family, education and many other areas of our lives.

Shostak believes that "compunications" represent a "major systems break, or a radical shift in the way fundamental institutions of society operate, such as the change from feudalism to capitalism. . . . Do we need to radically rethink the very goals of systematic education? Does the impact on American life appear likely to strengthen democracy?"(130). As we investigate the new technologies we should keep these questions in mind and evaluate the shock they suggest to our everyday lives.

What are the changes that are here or just over the horizon? Here are a few which will probably be superseded by others by the time you read this. First are listed those which are in operation now, and next are those which are theoretically possible but not yet in use:

Changes That are in Operation Now

> Computer-based pages of news and information. A "teletext" system employs a television signal for transmission. A "Viewdata" or a "Videotext" system uses a cable or telephone lines for transmission.
>
> On-line bibliographic data bases. Data bases consist of collections of records that can be called up by the use of a computer terminal. This information is displayed on the CRT (Cathode Ray Tube) screen of the computer. Some computers have the capacity also to print out the information on paper. Data bases are accessible through some thirty-nine on-line service suppliers (as of 1982).
>
> Full-text data bases. A complete encyclopedia is available in a data base.

The availability of an electronic *Readers Guide to Periodical Literature* covering twice the number of serials as the print edition.

More teachers devising their own computer programs, and students also engaging in this process.

Volunteers assisting in the use of computers, promoting the donation of computers to schools and working with students and teachers.

Great increase in the number of schools which have computers. As of 1982, it is estimated that one of every four school districts nationally has some kind of computer in use *for instructional purposes.*

The holdings of some school library media centers stored on computer memory space, the card catalog replaced by the computer, and on-line access terminals available for student and teacher use.

Circulation work performed by a computer. The light pen and the bar-code labels in use in public libraries for the past several years are now becoming a more common sight in school library media centers, too.

Expanded library networks. An individual who develops a computer program or data base can be connected into a network and so linked with a number of other people's systems. Thus the individual has access to enormous resources, and can be, within the network, both a user and supplier of information.

Many books being replaced by audio-tapes, video cassettes, and microforms.

In some schools children being taught to operate microcomputers beginning in the first grade, and older students being taught to design computer programs.

Teleconferences being transmitted by satellite.

Musical tapes and records stored in digital form allowing for reproduction by microcomputer.

Developments That are Projected and Possible but not yet in Common Use

It is projected that by 1990 a computer chip will contain ten million transistors.

On the horizon is the use of beams of electrons to build circuits of chemicals. The process is called molecular beam epitaxy.

With new chip designs, supercomputers will be built small enough and inexpensively enough to give one to each child as a personal learning tool.

Work is going forward on a refrigerated supercomputer with circuits which require only a grapefruit-sized volume of space. The machine can carry out ten times as many instructions per second as the current high-performance computers.

There will be classroom learning from talking computers.

Miniatured portable computers carried in your clothing or implanted in your brain.

A programmable hand-held computer with the power of today's most powerful computer.

A standardized protocol for access to data bases.

Disk antennas on housetops or front lawns to receive satellite transmissions. (A number of homes and institutions already have them.)

Interlibrary loan materials video transmitted.

Even more widespread use of home computers for student learning.

Widespread circulation of video cassettes and videotape players for home use by public libraries.

Laser-based audio disk recorders which will make record players obsolete.

The circulation of portable computers and programs for home use.

Portable language translators.

Introduction of software for computers that can be adapted to the way in which their owners organize and use information.

The designing of the library media specialist's office

with a central computer whose data base contains all of the information and records needed to organize materials and to administer the library media center. All data will be within arm's reach.

The availability by 1990 of a fifth-generation supercomputer which would process far greater amounts of data at superhigh speeds and also be able to act more human, capable of holding conversations, thinking logically and making common-sense judgments and decisions.

The projection of holographic images.

Bubble memory for storing larger amounts of data in a smaller space.

The use of the laser in the transmission of information.

And these developments merely scratch the surface. New possibilities and capabilities are surfacing daily.

In short, the computer, which has been used heretofore in libraries and in school systems on the whole for technical and administrative processes, is now moving very rapidly into intructional and management responsibilities. It has been fairly painless to accept and to appreciate the computer as a servant, quick and time-saving in performing routine tasks such as ordering, inventory, circulation processes, on-line reference, serials control, production of bibliographies, information retrieval and statistics and management reporting. The stress will mount as the computer becomes increasingly a colleague, to be seen perhaps as a rival or even a replacement in professional expertise. Library media personnel in all types of libraries will be at the eye of the storm, the heart of the change that this flood of "compunications" is bringing about. Small wonder then that stress is generated. But let's remember that the Chinese philosopher Kung Fu-tse (Confucius), in the sixth century B.C. said, "If man takes no thought about what is distant, he will find sorrow near at hand." Therefore, it would be wise to consider the communications and computer innovations that are coming and begin to plan now how to cope with them successfully. You don't really have any alternate course for action. It is a case of "shape up or ship out." Fortunately, all the changes won't strike at once and you will have time for gradual adjustment. But realizing that you must make that adjustment if you want to stay in your profession is a first step you can take now.

It will comfort you to know that some writers who have described the coming changes predict that the old media will survive. Byrne states, "As new media are added . . . we find that the old media are used more than ever"(27). Neill declares that "though computer terminals will have been added . . . and the card catalog replaced by small on-line access terminals . . . the book collections will still dominate"(106).

As you plan the coping strategies to inhibit stress and to make productive use of these technological changes, remember the basic survival strategies listed in the first chapter:

> Maintain an attitude of acceptance of change.
> Keep flexible.
> Evaluate your strengths and weaknesses.
> Strengthen your internal support by positive "self-talk."
> Learn self-relaxation skills.
> Work as a member of a team to implement effective use of new technologies.
> Develop external support by consulting those who have helped you in the past.
> Use experienced consultants.
> Read widely about the new technologies. Enroll in academic courses.
> Gain experience by finding opportunities to operate new equipment.

Other coping strategies which will put you in control of the situation and give you a feeling of self-worth are:

> Make the new technology a genuine part of the library rather than just stationing it in the library. Make it an integral part of the library media resources and tools.
> The parents and community members will need to be informed. Secure books and other materials for this purpose. Purchase "How You Can Learn to Live with Computers" by Harry

Kleinbert, Lippincott, or in paper from Penquin, 1978.

Buy or borrow, but be sure to read and study one or more of these other good and recent books:

Broadbeer, Robin, Peter de Bono and Peter Laurie. *Beginner's Guide to Computers.* Reading, Mass: Addison Wesley, 1982.

Greenblatt, Stanley. *Understanding Computers by Common Sense.* New York: Simon and Schuster, 1983.

Garret, Mark. *Bits, Bytes and Buzzwords.* Beaverton, Ore.: Dilithium Press, 1983

McCaled, Robert. *Small Business Computer Principles.* Beaverton, Ore.: Dilithium Press, 1982.

Willis, Jerry and Merl Miller. *Computers for Everybody,* 2nd ed. Beaverton, Ore.: Dilithium Press, 1982

Subscribe to "ComputerTown USA." Order from ComputerTown International, P.O. Box E, Menlo Park, CA 94025.

Become familiar with available data bases so that you can advise computer terminal users.

Keep in control of the new technology in the media center. Monitor its use and evaluate its effectiveness. Establish objectives.

Get involved in the selection of new hardware and software. Learn how to evaluate video programs. Survey the software available for a certain microcomputer before purchase.

Software for a given microcomputer is generally not interchangeable (compatible) with that of a different brand of microcomputer. Criteria for evaluating software:

Documentation (instructions on how to use— clear, concise, easy to read).

Ease of use—different formats, cassette tapes, diskettes, cartridges, ease of loading.

Audience—appropriate content.

Suitable for library setting—creates a rowdy response?
Error handling—make certain program is "bomb proof."
Overall presentation—useful? fulfills purpose? user in control? written for your specific microcomputer? (See Appendix F for software review sources.)
Participate in a library network. Secure from the Government Printing Office a copy of the final report of the Task Force on the Role of the School Library Media Program in the National Network. Study this and help implement the recommendations.

As you develop your strategy of coping with the change to new technologies, you need to recognize the problems associated with them, especially with computers. These problems can be summarized as follows:

A time lag exists in schools. This is due to budget constraints, resistance to change, and fear of innovation.
The attitudes of some library media specialists inhibit the development of networking. They are unwilling to share, to plan with others, to communicate, or to adjust or compromise.
There is a lack of adequate software.
There is a danger that libraries will be perceived solely as the place for books, and some other location as the place for computers and their materials. You would be wise to stake your claim to interest and expertise *now*, if you have not already done so, so that you are recognized in your building and system as a leader in all information handling and retrieval by whatever method.
A large segment of the population, including the undereducated and the poor, might be discriminated against due to the cost of computer use (a charge per hour), and also to the lack of skills

needed for effective use: manual, visual and cognitive skills, including literacy.

There is a hazard of "information pollution," a term which reflects the ease with which errors may be compounded with computer use. Inaccurate data may become part of a permanent file to which other data bases refer in building their own bases.

The new technologies are devised to make work easy, and yet we cling to the ethic that working hard is the key to success. The fact is that computers will force people to work hard but to "work smarter" and thereby raise the level of many job requirements.

Unauthorized access to personal data might endanger privacy and enhance the possibility of "big brother" surveillance. (This was a term coined by George Orwell in his 1949 book, *Nineteen Eighty-Four*, which forecast in astonishing detail the effects of, and problems created by, computer technology.)

There is a danger of information overload.

The new technologies in school library media centers might cause some loss of attention to basic goals and humanistic values.

There is some concern that extensive use of computers for learning will cause students to ignore those aspects of a subject which are not included in a data base because they cannot be programmed. Affective learning and that which depends upon feelings and interaction with people may suffer unless particular efforts are made to counteract these effects.

The use of computers affords a great opportunity for fraud, embezzlement and trespass.

False, misleading or inadequate information can be widely disseminated through computers and other electronic means.

Copyright laws need to be revised to reflect the use of the new technologies.

Long use of the Cathode Ray Tube screen causes

vision problems.

Extensive use of computers may cause students to become more isolated from their peer group and result in a decrease in social and community interaction.

There is a danger that computer programs will be perceived as entertainment only. You need to become knowledgeable about the elements of programs which facilitate learning. Zamora quotes Marshall McLuhan; "Those who draw a distinction between Education and Entertainment don't know the first thing about either"(163).

One final problem is perceived by Scanlon: "Computer literacy is a prerequisite to participation in an information society and as much a social obligation as reading literacy.... Schools are not keeping pace.... Our kids are with their television, microcomputers, their video tape recorders, pocket calculators, digital clocks ... they are lucky to find one terminal in a school building and usually only teachers and counselors can use it. We have a fast-learning child in a slow-moving institution"(124). Shostak agrees with this analysis, and advocates "the development of an education system which would guarantee all Americans ownership or free access to home computers, community learning centers, and all the materials of educational technology"(130).

There has in fact been a move in Congress to achieve this by providing tax breaks for companies who present computers to schools as gifts.

You will be aware of these problem areas as you implement your stress-relieving plan. You will be wise to join your efforts with those of others to solve these problems and others which may arise. You will begin now to meld the new technologies you already have with other library media resources to provide innovative, exciting instructional options. Above all, you will focus your efforts on staying on top of the waves of change rather than letting yourself be inundated and swamped by them.

STRESS-CREATING SITUATION

Your middle school has purchased three microcomputers for the library media center from a company which sent a representative to demonstrate their operation and use. Although you've learned to operate these microcomputers, you are very apprehensive about their use in the library media center in terms of confusion they may cause, discipline problems or directing attention from other tasks at hand. You've purchased programs for instruction in mathematics and language arts skills and a few games which have learning possibilities.

STRESS-REDUCTION RESPONSE

After considering any side effects, which of the following would you choose as the most effective alternative?

1. You discuss your concerns and problems with a close friend in the school who has always been very supportive. You use positive "self-talk" to strengthen your self-confidence.
2. You limit the use of the microcomputers by keeping them in the equipment room out of sight.
3. You read about how other schools use them and visit some of these schools.
4. You ask the principal to appoint a committee of teachers, parents and students to work with you on developing guidelines for the use of the microcomputers, and ways they can contribute to the instructional program.
5. You ask the principal to arrange with a knowledgeable consultant for a workshop for the faculty on the use of microcomputers.
6. As you plan instructional units with teachers you treat the microcomputer programs as one of the library media center's resources which you suggest along with other materials.

11
CHANGES IN THE STUDENT BODY

Some library media specialists have had to survive the sudden influx of students quite different from those they had been accustomed to dealing with. Other school faculties will have to face this strain and the stress it will create in the future. There are three categories of these students which will be discussed here:

> Those who are from cultural and ethnic minorities, including non-English speaking.
> Those with mental and physical handicaps.
> Those with standards of behavior and values that are at odds with those of most middle-class professionals and the majority of the other children.

Some of you will doubt your capacity to help develop the learning potential of these students. You may feel inadequate and defeated by the difficulty of communicating with them. On the other hand, you may have such a strong commitment to the ideal of reaching out to all children in an accepting and positive way that you will find your experience of working with these particular groups of young people to be challenging and satisfying.

Let's consider those who are culturally and ethnically different from those with whom you have been used to working. How can you offer them the programs they need? First, in order to develop an understanding of them and their cultures, you should read widely and consult those who are experienced in working with them. Next, you should take active steps to meet the problem. You must develop new attitudes, new methods and new programs. Remember that we can learn much from these students, and you will want to give them an opportunity to contribute to activities. Watt reminds us that "programs developed by or about culturally or ethnically different students would be of value for *all* students"(154).

As you become better informed you learn more about the special needs of these students, such as the need for intensive help with reading problems, and the need for opportunities to develop a positive self-identity and belief in their own capabilities and potentials as students. They need resources to help them to cope with real-life problems and materials on mental health, physical fitness, proper nutrition, drug abuse. Watt gives a list of activities to provide motivation for the use of materials on these and other subjects.(154)

You probably plan such activities for all students, but with these students especially you will want to emphasize wholesome intercultural relationships, promote participation, and accept their contributions through role playing, dramatization, play discussions, media production, debates, choral reading and peer teaching.

Other ideas include:

> A "Skill Exchange." For example, a student exchanges his/her reading skill for help with mathematics.
> A figure control/physical development display with a student giving demonstrations along with the media display.
> A "Budget Beauty Bar" consisting of health and beauty aids made from inexpensive substances.
> An "Economy Chef's Shelf" with cookbooks for nutritious, inexpensive meals.
> A "Babysitter's Survival Kit" containing first-aid information, emergency phone numbers, quiet

games and activities, checklist for the child's safety and the safety of the sitter.
Resources on family life and marriage.
Student-made slide-tape on comparison shopping which gives the comparative cost of popular items from different sources.
Participation in the library media center's student-assistant club. This helps develop a sense of responsibility and self-pride.

If you have a bilingual program in your school you can learn much about methods and materials by conferring with the teachers who are specialists in this area. Ask the students whose native language is not English to help you develop special displays about their countries and/or cultures. Interfile materials for them with those in the general collection.

Particularly valuable for the cultural and ethnic minority students are your efforts to promote appreciation of art and beauty representing many types of cultures—Western, Eastern, primitive and sophisticated. Have available framed reproductions of famous and lesser-known works of art and resources about artists. Invite guest artists to make presentations.

As you learn more about Afro-American, Hispanic, Southeast Asian, American Indian and other histories and cultures work with teachers to integrate materials about them with the content of their disciplines.

As you implement your program to meet the needs of the students in these groups, you will find that your tension will diminish, you will become more comfortable in working with them and you will begin to enjoy the experience. The catalyst in all these activities will be your warm, accepting, caring attitude toward these students.

Another group of students we are concerned with are those with mental and physical handicaps. When Public Law 94-142, Education for All Handicapped Children, was passed in 1975, the result was that many of these children were brought out of the self-contained special education classrooms and "mainstreamed," or placed in the regular classrooms with other children. The swiftness with which this change came about found teachers and media specialists with no competencies and no special training for the job rather suddenly working with these exceptional children. As a result, library media specialists and teachers were often frustrated, felt deficient, and suffered various degrees of stress.

One remedy for this is to take a positive attitude toward your responsibilities for these children, to get to know them and to understand both their handicaps and their abilities. Here again, your attitude is crucial to success in working with them. Warm understanding, patience and unquenchable belief in them and in yourself are needed. They need an extra supply of love, support and encouragement. Fast echoes the thoughts often expressed in the literature about exceptional children: "Remember that they are children and have the same needs as everyone else for love and affection, for positive experiences for self-development and for people to help them"(44).

After you have upgraded your knowledge about these students, and talked with their parents and with those who are experienced in working with them, you are ready to participate in planning their educational experiences. An individualized education plan should be developed jointly by a qualified school official, the child's teacher, the parents and the child, if possible. You play an active role in finding and applying the information needed to work with these children and in suggesting suitable library-media related activities. (See Appendix G for list of organizations which supply materials and information.)

In addition to their greater-than-usual need for understanding patience and affection, these children require:

Emphasis on language arts, especially reading.
Materials that meet their interest and maturity levels and help them to enhance their capabilities and compensate for their disabilities.
Help in making and keeping friends, working with their peers and being accepted.
Physical facilities that make materials and equipment accessible.
Help in working with parents, teachers and others in authority.
Help in developing skills of creative thinking, skills such as anticipating events, seeing cause and effect relationships, communication, planning and decision-making.

Extra individual help.

As the library media specialist you have four major roles:
1. To help the handicapped students themselves to develop competencies and skills to enable them to function in society.
2. To help dispel among the other children the stereotypes about handicapped people by creating awareness of, and taking every opportunity to highlight, the capabilities and talents of many handicapped which are often developed outstandingly by way of compensation for their disabilities.
3. To be especially sensitive to and supportive of the efforts of teachers to provide for the special needs of handicapped students.
4. To bridge the gap between home and school by providing help to teachers and parents in working together on behalf of handicapped students. Purchase materials that will enable parents to reinforce the learning that takes place in school and make parents welcome in the library media center.

In securing materials you will probably use the standard selection criteria, but bear in mind also that there are a number of sources of excellent materials especially prepared for both mentally and physically handicapped students. (See Appendix G.) In addition, consider the following:

Children with muscular dystrophy are unable to handle heavy books. In general, orthopedically handicapped children like paperbacks because they are easy to handle.

For the physically handicapped in your school, make available books about people who have excelled despite their handicaps in a variety of sports, the dance and other activities.

Purchase cassette tapes rather than reel-to-reel tapes, as they are easier to manipulate.

Secure easy-to-read materials with simple sentence structure and concepts. Stories should have plenty of repetition and many illustrations. Remember that a short attention span is characteristic of many handicapped children.

Purchase filmstrips with captions for the deaf.

Printed materials for the partially sighted must have suitable format, a good type size, spacing and ink and paper that lends itself to easy reading.

Provide educational components for programs to which blind students can listen on the radio, and encourage local stations to air more such programs (which can be shared by blind adults in the community also).

Try to find funds to purchase the World Book Encyclopedia in braille, and be certain that visually handicapped students and their families have access to all varieties of special materials and equipment with which to use it. For example, Talking Books are available from state library agencies for those who are blind or partially sighted.

Consider recordings with compressed speech (speeded-up recordings without voice or speech distortion), on which organizations for the blind will have information.

Infantino(72) and Metcalf(102) offer some of the following suggestions for a library media program for exceptional children:

Show captioned films or nonverbal films.

Offer story hours in sign language. If you have not learned to sign, a teacher or parent can sign while you tell the story.

Use films, slides, filmstrips, transparencies and the flannel-board in story telling. Be sure to face the children with the light on your face.

Have puppet and drama shows.

Involve parents in your program.

Promote the Talking Book program (stories and whole books on tapes or records).

Show children how to produce nonprint materials. Let deaf children use the 35mm camera to record their perception of their environment.

Provide a wide variety of materials.
Have programs which use poetry and choral readings.
Use carrels for self-instruction with slides and synchronized tape cartridges for auditory training. Rear-screen-projection cabinets with 8mm projectors are useful.
Teach one library skill or concept at a time followed by review exercises. Repeat a statement two or three different ways. Use visual materials.

Support teachers and parents in their efforts. You will find that your determination to provide a sound program for exceptional children will be "bread upon the waters." Your stress will disappear as you learn to admire and learn from the courage, perseverance and unique qualities of the students who are culturally and ethnically different and those who are mentally and physically handicapped. You will come to treasure their friendship and affection.

The third category of students—those with unacceptable standards of behavior and values—are not a clearly defined group. They may be found anywhere in the student body. These students have one or more of the following characteristics:

They are disrespectful to teachers and other adults.
They use foul language.
They have no visible motivation to learn, and are often disruptive in the school library media center.
They have no compunction about lying, cheating or stealing.
They disregard the rights of others.
They are often involved in conflicts with others in their peer group.

Some believe that this behavior, as a reflection of society's increasing permissiveness, its breakdown of family ties, its increase in violent crime, its corruption in government and business, and its decline in moral standards, is almost impossible to do anything about. The majority of citizens, however, expect the public schools to promote acceptable behavior and desirable values, but there is no consensus on the most effective instructional methods, even among educators who have spent years studying the subject. There is agreement on the fact that the desirable way to instill high standards and acceptable values is to provide opportunities for students to experience these in their everyday lives, in school, home and community.

Martin and Sargent list the ways in which the library media specialist can contribute to this process(99):

1. Provide for development of positive self-concepts by
    displaying student work and giving recognition to student achievements,
    providing an environment in the library media center which fosters positive attitudes,
    exemplifying fairness, integrity and justice in dealing with students.
2. Promote responsible behavior by
    encouraging self-directed study and research,
    assigning meaningful jobs to students in the library media center,
    seeking student opinions regarding materials acquisitions,
    seeking student ideas for solving such problems as book loss, vandalism.
3. Demonstrate desirable values by
    encouraging respect for rights of others in the use of resources and materials in the center,
    encouraging respect for competency and efficiency,
    demonstrating open-minded consideration of issues,
    providing models of moral behavior through reading materials.

It is important to assess, if possible, the home situations of these students, including parental attitudes toward them, and involve parents in remedial approaches, if this seems likely to be productive. Family and school in concerted, cooperative action can offset, to some extent at least, bad community and neighborhood influences.

Most important of all, you should in all your actions and words try to be a model of high ethical standards and commendable values.

Though at first you may experience stress in trying to work with these students, if you accept the challenge of helping them develop more acceptable life-styles and follow a constructive course of action, you will find that as your interest in such activities increases your stress will recede before your feeling of accomplishment.

Stress-Creating Situation

You are very nervous and unsure of yourself when students with mental and physical disabilities are first "mainstreamed" at your middle school. But you follow the advice of their teachers and offer some programs designed especially for them. However, there is one child with muscular dystrophy who is very apathetic and doesn't respond to any group activities. This child evidently needs a great deal of individual attention.

Stress-Reduction Response

After considering any side effects, which of the following would your choose as the most effective alternative?

1. You tell the child's teacher about his lack of response and let her work with him.
2. You learn from the child's teacher that he has been neglected by his family. You invite his mother to come to the library media center and introduce her to some materials you have purchased for parents.
3. You read about muscular dystrophy and its effects and order special materials for him.
4. You ask his teacher to let her aide bring him to the library media center and you summon all your resources of patience, understanding and affection to work with him. You talk with him about his interests, select several poems, and help him read them. You help him make transparencies to illustrate the

ones he liked, using the color-lift process. You type the poems and duplicate them on acetate sheets to be used with the illustrations, then invite his mother to come and see his accomplishment.

12
CHANGES IN THE CURRICULUM AND SCHOOL ORGANIZATION

You have been fine-tuning the library media program so that it meets the demands of the existing curriculum when suddenly you have discovered that a new emphasis will be introduced in all subject areas. No one told you this was in the offing; possibly it is one of those changes mandated "from above." The focus might be on environmental education, or it might be on human interdependence or on economic education. This adds a new dimension to your planning with teachers, to your selection of materials, to your recommendations for student activities and to the whole library media program. You are supposed to be all ready to implement this almost immediately. This creates stress, and your stress is compounded if, in addition, you find that the administration has decided on a different mode of organizing students for learning, such as modular scheduling, team teaching, open classes or computer-assisted instruction. Your salvation will lie in the extent to which you have learned stress reduction skills, and the degree to which you have learned to "shift gears" smoothly.

Since to be forewarned is to be forearmed, let us take a look at what eminent scholars and educators are predicting will be instructional trends in the future. Reisler quotes from the report of the President's Commission for a National Agenda for the Eighties: "A successful education system would assure that every student obtains the basic skills and social experience required to become a functional and productive citizen in a democratic society"(116).

But what kind of society will students face in the future for which the schools must equip them? Shane examines the *Global 2000 Report to the President*, mentioned in chapter IX, and cites aspects of this future world envisioned in the report of a panel of 135 distinguished scholars:

> Pressures from the one hundred thirty or so nonindustrial "developing" countries against the twenty-nine or thirty industrial "developed" countries.
> Increased population and hunger.
> Resource depletion and pollution.
> Dangers in sophisticated weaponry and the prospect of additional nuclear accidents.
> European and U.S. democracies under increasing stress due to pressures for entitlements, and the resistance of self-interest groups which are becoming less tolerant.
> The evil trio of worldwide inflation, increasing public and private debt, and unemployment.
> The electronic assault on human reason made by the media and spearheaded by television(128).

Combs looks at the future more from the point of view of individual student development(34). He describes four certainties:

> Certainty I   The information explosion. Technical information doubles every ten years.
> Certainty II   The increasing pace of change. Today's students may have to change life work four or five times.
> Certainty III The primacy of the impact of social problems on human interdependence. Students must learn to live effectively with themselves and other people.
> Certainty IV Personal fulfillment increasingly important. Those who feel thwarted and hostile are a danger to everyone. Providing for basic needs frees people to seek fulfillment of personal goals.

What do these views of a future turbulent world prescribe for curriculum change? Shane lists some curriculum goals(128):

Educated beings will have
 developed humane values,
 pride in achievement whether in mind or hand,
 learned the meaning of social responsibility,
 the desire to be of use to themselves and to
  the world community,
 learned the meaning of ethical interpersonal
  relationships.

Ornstein believes that major changes in society and education are likely to influence curriculum, and names four features of the future curriculum(109).

1. Communications capacity will occur at an accelerating rate. There will be a rapid increase of students learning at computer terminals in their homes or at a publicly supported neighborhood learning center.

2. Lifelong learning will occur increasingly outside the traditional school as people are forced to prepare for second or third careers or to meet personal goals. Business and industry as well as community educational resources will provide for much continuing learning.

3. An understanding of other nations and cultures and international cooperation must be developed. Greater interdependency among peoples is fostered by telecommunication satellites, the energy crisis, supersonic airlines and multinational corporations.

4. There is a danger that human values will be subordinated to technological advances. When planning a curriculum to make use of new technologies for learning any perceived gains must be weighed against consequences as to social and psychological development of students.

Other suggestions for the future curriculum:

The curriculum must become increasingly personal and individual.

Students need to have information to help them to confront real problems, in school and community, including personal problems.

Schools must meet society's requirements for skilled workers in new fields.

Students must be educated to be problem solvers, to be able to weigh alternatives and to make good choices.

Students must not lose sight of historical perspective, nor the perspectives and insights afforded by the arts and literature.

Among recommendations for different ways for schools to organize students for learning:

Make provision for students to learn at home with computers. Devise learning contracts with these students.

Provide time for students to intern with a business.

Share human resources and unused facilities with businesses or community agencies, and in turn benefit from the expertise of their personnel and the loan of materials and equipment.

Schedule classes so that teachers can plan more interdisciplinary and multidisciplinary approaches.

Since students learn differently and at various rates, and since computers are now available for record-keeping, organize schools for more individualized instruction.

Much has been written about the requirement for a changed curriculum and school organization to meet the needs of students in a changing world. However, Ornstein calls our attention to the fact that many innovations of the last three decades had been introduced and dropped after a short time. Curriculum and instruction remained the same, "reliance on textbooks, teacher dominated activities, students being quiet, following directions, copying from the blackboard or workbook, memorizing information which the teacher provides"(109). Ornstein observes that Brandwein and Goodlad agree with his evaluation of scant school change. They visited hundreds of classes, Brandwein in 1960 and Goodlad in 1969 and again in 1979. (A book reporting Goodlad's findings and recommendations was published under the title *A Place Called School* by McGraw Hill in 1983.) Reisler, too, states that "the structure and operation of schools changed very little in response to altered needs of students"(116).

Though curriculum and school organization innovations have not been widely sustained in the past, the library media specialist has the qualifications to be a major factor in their success in the future. As Sullivan points out, the "library media specialist has broad professional preparation in education and in media. As such, he/she understands learning theory, educational psychology, growth and development, and curriculum in addition to media selection, production, utilization, and administration"(135).

There are two reasons why you should become involved in any new curriculum proposals or new approaches to learning: first, your input might increase students' chances to be better prepared for a changing world; and second, this activity will help counteract any stress you might be feeling because of apprehension that proposed innovations will necessitate changes in your library media procedures and program. It might be difficult for you to participate in curricular planning, implementation and evaluation because many administrators are not aware that this is an appropriate part of your role, and teachers may feel that this is solely their territory and it is being invaded. Though you might have problems in this area, some appropriate degree of assertiveness may be in order here. Grazier, while making a survey of research analyzing the role of the library media specialist, found that one researcher felt that "media specialists must accept their enlarged role or lose it to others less qualified"(57) (See Appendix H for planning curriculum units.)

The urgent need for school library media specialists to make certain that the specific aspects of the role of the library media program in implementing educational reform is made clear to their own administrators and communities was pointed up by the publication in 1983 of *A Nation At Risk,* the report of the National Commission on Excellence in Education. Although this report made many recommendations, and suggested actions necessary to their implementation relating to motivation, study skills, learning materials and their content, and teaching methods (among others), *School library media centers and programs were not even cited as being involved in this implementation process.* Disheartening though this may seem, it presents the opportunity for every school library media specialist to discuss with principal, subject and curriculum coordinators, teachers and parents, the vital potential role of the library media program in upgrading instruction.

Other stress-reducing activities include the following:

> Read and learn all you can about a proposed instructional innovation.
>
> Suggest to your administrator that a consultant with experience in that area be invited to the school to hold a workshop for the faculty.
>
> Visit one or more schools which have put the innovation into operation.
>
> Attend academic workshops or enroll in courses on the subject.
>
> Request that all those who will be affected by the curricular change be involved in the process: administrators, supervisors, teachers, parents and learners, as well as you and your staff.
>
> Identify, select, and evaluate relevant learning resources, some in the library media collection and others to be added to it or obtained through the interlibrary loan network from another library or libraries.
>
> Plan learning activities to implement objectives.
>
> Provide in-service education activities for teachers and for your staff.
>
> Sharpen your leadership skills. (See Appendix I for a discussion of leadership skills.)
>
> Develop learning packages and set up individual learning centers.
>
> Encourage different modes of student use of materials, individual and small group as well as whole class.
>
> Promote flexible media skills instruction coordinated with units of study.
>
> Give students the freedom to inquire, to discover, to

choose, and to practice self-selection and self-direction.

Exercise your most proficient interpersonal skills.

Communicate often and in diverse ways.

Make yourself a valued member of the team working on the proposed curricular or school organization change.

Collaborate with teachers to
identify learning alternatives,
evaluate materials according to students' needs and learning styles,
supervise the production of additional resources,
help students design and produce materials in all formats,
assist in the evaluation of learning alternatives and effective use of media.

In all your activities focus on the individual learner, his needs, his interests and his abilities.

Exhibit flexibility of mind. Be accessible, approachable, responsive and helpful.

Whatever confronts you in the future, whether it is global education, education for parenting, computer literacy in the curricular area, independent study by interactive video, nongraded classes, or differentiated staffing in the school organization area, if you can apply the above survival strategies and remain calm, self-assured, and in control, you will have conquered stress.

STRESS-CREATING SITUATION

Your high school principal decides to offer a course in consumer education for tenth-grade students. Since no one has experience with such a course there is much tension among the faculty.

STRESS-REDUCTION RESPONSE

After considering any side effects, which of the following would you choose as the most effective alternative?

1. You decide to reduce your tension by not getting involved and by waiting until someone requests a service.
2. You limit your cooperation to purchasing additional materials for student use and professional materials on the topic for the teachers.
3. You discuss your concerns with the district and state library media consultants.
4. You find a description of a consumer education course in a professional book and show it to the principal.
5. You decide to assume a leadership role. You ask the principal if he would approve a team approach if teachers are willing. You secure the participation of the science, social studies, mathematics and English teachers. Together with these, you plan the objectives of the course, select student activities, identify materials, and outline evaluation procedures. All of you support each other and develop a warm working relationship, as well as an effective consumer education course.

13
Changes in Financial Support

Public education is slowly being starved of the resources needed to honor the historic United States commitment to universally available free education and equality of opportunity. This condition prevails regardless of the fact that, as McLoone states, there has been a sixfold growth in the cost of all education since 1959(94). Public education's financial problems arise from decreased purchasing power due to inflation, reduction in funds because of declines in enrollment and direct budget cuts. In one school district where the regular program budget had increased by 56% since 1971-72, utilities costs during this period rose by 245%, transportation by 221% and total salaries by 79%. The rate of inflation for the period was 110%. In order to survive, this school district cut 30% of its staff positions, closed 27% of its buildings, cut the budget for purchasing audio-visual equipment by 75%, and cut supplies and materials 25%.

These reductions were particularly hard to bear since from 1956 to 1976 public education had been adequately financed. During those years, every state enacted major tax increases and the rates or coverage of existing taxes were raised at least three times in every state. But since 1977, eighteen states have enacted some type of ceiling on tax collections and spending. At this time the economy was in recession, and taxpayers demanded property-tax relief and limits on taxation for all services and on all government spending. For the first time in history, in 1978-79, state revenues were proportionately more important in the support of education than were local revenues. State income and sales taxes have replaced a portion of local property taxes. The federal government has never been a major source of revenue for education finance, and in 1979 the National Education Association estimated that the federal government provided just 9% of education funds for local schools. However, it should be noted that these federal funds, through a small factor percentage-wise, provide for most of the innovative directions and programs, as well as for equalization of learning opportunities for the children of poor communities and states, and remedial/compensatory programs.

Lewis warns that "Public education's increasing dependence on state money brings added pressures and greater demands for accountability"(88). This has led to various tests and measurements of student learning which, unfortunately, all too often reduce learning expectations—for literacy, as a prime example—to the most basic functional level and lose sight of higher literacy requirements. Competency tests for teachers also too often test for the wrong things, and mandated local advisory committees become mere rubber stamps for poor performance or platforms for single-issue pressures upon administrators. Fuhrman believes that "Educators may realize that renewed organization and action at the state level is the only way to survive the tough battle over the disappearing dollar"(50), and, it might be added, an apparently growing lack of public confidence in the schools.

At the state level, educators find themselves embroiled in controversies between wealthy districts and poor ones, urban/rural tensions, and conflicts between special needs programs and the operation of basic instructional programs. During the 1970s there began to be a shift to educational decision-making by governors, their staff education experts and legislatures, rather than by educators.

As adequate funding is slowly eroded, Pinckney(111), Fuhrman(50), and Reisler(110) make a strong case for the necessity of providing sufficient financing for the urban schools with their concentration of culturally deprived, poor and minority children. Pinckney warns that "failing miserably to provide meaningful education programs for literally millions of inner-city and even rural children ... all levels of government are likely to end up spending billions to support them as adults or when they drop out of school." This is a frightening prospect with a cost to individuals and to society which cannot even be stated in monetary terms.

Library media specialists must join, indeed *lead*, other educators in mounting a massive campaign, supported by private-sector interests, to make the public aware that it is in society's self-interest to rekindle concern and support for the education of minorities and the culturally deficient and isolated. The widespread growth among these populations will make them much more visible, powerful and dominant in the future.

A report of the Carnegie Council on Children, published in 1981, shows that the number of children under age fifteen had dropped in the decade since 1970 by about 25%. Meanwhile, the twenty-five to thirty-four-year-olds and those sixty-five and over have increased by about 30% and 20%, respectively. What this means, according to some educators, is that as adults in the future, today's shrunken population of children will have to provide the nation's productive force, support an enormous number of the elderly and, at the same time, rear their own children. Moreover, with proportionately higher fertility rates among minority groups, a much greater portion of this productive force will be recruited from the predominantly low-income, minority, urban populations. These groups are perceived and perceive themselves as being inferior socially and technoeconomically, and the schools transfer this status into inferior education, according to the Carnegie Council. This situation is described by Ogbu as a caste barrier: "So long as caste remains the principle of social organization, no efforts to use the schools to equalize the social and occupational status of different minority and majority castes can succeed because the social system demands that both desirable and undesirable occupational positions be filled on an ascriptive basis. The schools therefore continue to prepare a disproportionate number of lower-caste groups for their traditional menial positions, although they may not do this consciously"(108). Programs which seek to change school policies and practices so that their goal is the development of new attitudes and skills for minorities are a necessary component of the strategy to eliminate caste barriers.

School library media specialists need to recognize and accept their role in initiating and implementing programs to raise the sights of minority children and improve their sense of self-worth, and to help them become motivated, literate and competent. (See suggestions in chapter XI.)

Kirst lists the social and political trends affecting funding for public education, included here because library media specialists need so much to be informed and reminded of them so that they are in a position to plan possible countervailing actions(78).

> 1. Enrollment decline. This is expected to be 17% in the twenty-year period 1970-1990. The decline is expected to be more extensive in the northeast and north-central states and less in the south and west. This is due largely to the migration of families following jobs to these regions.
> 2. Loss of voter support. Gallup polls taken in 1969 and again in 1981 showed a 15% decrease in the number of respondents who said they would favor raising taxes for public schools. There are several contributing factors in this. First, the negative view of public education in the media has alienated some voters. (Opposition to integration and busing has turned many of the conservative elements against the public schools generally, and has resulted in tremendous growth of small independent schools.) Second, and even more significant, the number of people with school age children is declining: three in five voters in 1952, as compared with one in five voters in 1982. In areas where the ratio is greater, the population tends to be low-income or immigrant without sufficient political power to increase budgets that would benefit their children. Children of these families often need costly special programs unpopular with voters. Finally, the political power of the people with no direct stake in education, especially senior citizens, is growing daily with their numbers.

3. Decrease in federal aid. Now there is more competition for scarce federal funds, and by 1982 education had been virtually declared not to be a national priority or even a national issue at all.*
4. The end of specialized programs. Health education, even drug abuse, counseling, and other important programs in addition to library media programs will be slated for elimination. The use of computers will be increasingly popular, "thus avoiding the need to add media specialists." *Note well this erroneous belief.*

*Author's footnote: In 1983, thanks largely to repercussions from the aforementioned report on excellence (or the lack of it), education became a highly visible political issue, but no increase in federal support for it was being recommended.

To offset these trends, Kirst advises teachers to become a militant force focusing their attention on political power at the state level with a special push in primary races for the state legislature. The development of strong lobbies is also recommended, as well as teacher-led public-relations campaigns to focus on the concerns of teachers and to try to reverse the low public esteem for education. Also, educators should realize the value of making alliances both within and outside of their own ranks. The involvement of labor and business in public education should be sought. You can participate in these activities and you should, because when it comes to cuts, you and your interests are right up there on the firing line. School library media programs almost surely will experience these cuts unless you work hard at bringing home to people the centrality of education and libraries to the community's and the country's well-being, and to their personal success as individuals.

Gone are the days—for the time being, at least—when almost all Americans, perhaps *especially* the poor and underclasses, recognized the truth of and subscribed to such sentiments as those of the unknown author who said;

> I am Education. I bear the torch that enlightens the world, fires the imagination, and feeds the flames of genius. I give wings to dreams and might to brawn and brain. I am the parent of progress, the

creator of culture and the molder of destiny.... I banish ignorance, discourage vice, disarm anarchy. Thus I become freedom's citadel, the arm of democracy.... The school is my workshop; here I stir ambitions, stimulate ideals, forge the keys that open the door to opportunity, the master of human destiny. I am the source of inspiration, the aid of aspiration, for I am Irresistible Power.

Restoring the sense that education generally, and libraries and books as its most enduring symbols, spell hope and enhancement for people of all classes, races and economic levels should be an underlying constant theme of all your lobbying and support-building activities.

Benson[17] also endorses activities directed at state legislatures and suggests that the focus be placed on the *successes* that the schools enjoy. In addition, he urges the possibility of creative financing arranged by administrators who have acquired sufficient knowledge of federal and state laws and accounting practices. He believes that administrators can and should become more proficient in management techniques involving the use of the computer. Benson also advocates looking into the possibility of expanding job preparation programs in schools in terms of specific industries.

You are probably already only too well aware of the ways in which cutbacks in public education will affect the library media center and its programs: reduced support and professional staff; severely restricted funds for materials and equipment; and programs curtailed or eliminated. The "most unkindest cut of all" is, of course, the elimination of your own position.

Three key words in relation to defending your program against unwarranted cuts—those that are out of line with the cuts made in other programs, and those that will seriously disrupt the ability of the library media program to serve instructional needs—are *awareness, alertness* and *action*.

You must be aware of what is happening and completely informed about the school district budgeting process, what steps it goes through and where the key intervention points are. Attend budget hearings and other Board of Education meetings at which budget matters are to be discussed. If you are sufficiently alert, you will be able to see cuts coming your way and may be able to head them off or be prepared to fight them. It pays to know whether the cuts slated or proposed for your program are proportionate to those proposed for other programs, or whether the library media programs have been thoughtlessly (usually ignorantly) considered to be merely "supplemental" rather than central to instruction and thus expendable.

You must, of couse, have programs that are worth defending, and demonstrably so. If the library media program of which you have charge is productive of learning, developed in cooperation with teachers and truly important to students, many other people in the community will know this besides yourself. Be sure that they know when action and advocacy is needed. When enough people turn out to fight for a library media program they really admire and want, budget trimmers nearly always can find something else to cut.

Breed(22) and Heller and Montgomery(66) suggest that the following actions be taken when facing cuts in the library media program:

1. Collect statistics. When you first hear that the board is considering economy measures, you had better begin collecting these statistics:
   Circulation figures (spot-check once a month).
   Number of students coming to the library
      media center (also periodic spot-checks).
   Data on media center holdings (provides
      rationale for adequate staff).
   Data on time-study analysis for specific job
      tasks.
   Number of students and teachers using each
      library media program, and staff
      needed to maintain each.
2. Have on hand job descriptions for each media staff position.
3. Get teachers to endorse, by signed petition, programs threatened with elimination. Also get student endorsement.
4. Ask parents to verify their chidren's gains as a result of library media center activities.

5. Contact professional organizations for library and media services to give authoritative testimony regarding program benefits.
6. Quote from the accreditation organization's requirements for library media services. In some states withdrawal of accreditation means loss of state funds.
7. Describe the central role of the library media center in the total school program:
   It is an integral part of the academic program.
   It serves all curricular areas. A cut in media
      services affects all teachers and the
      quality of the instructional program.
   It is a source of support for teachers when
      other cuts force an increase in class
      sizes and loss of teacher aides.

Living with the possibility of cuts in the library media program is a stressful enough situation for you, but if the cuts are actually made you have a severe problem and must activate your stress-reduction strategies. The fact that you made an active response by working to avert the cuts is a plus for you. Also, you will want to practice positive "self-talk" and relaxation skills. Next, consider your options in priority order and choose your continuing course of action. List the steps to be taken. You will have to reduce the time spent with students and teachers so that you can take care of clerical duties, if your clerk is cut. One library media specialist reported a dilemma. Should she complete the clerical tasks after school hours and on weekends? If she does, the administrator might think that she didn't need a clerk after all. If she doesn't, the teachers and students will suffer from curtailment of programs.(66)

If a special reading program is eliminated, explain to the students and let them take some of the materials home to use as best they can. Solicit teacher help when possible. Increase the volunteer program. (See Appendix D for information on the volunteer program.)

Streamline your purely routine and technical duties and spend as little time on them as possible.

Continue and step up your public relations program. Use a multi-media presentation at parent/teacher meetings and at community club meetings.

Get statements from teachers, students and parents on the results of the cuts. Summarize these and publicize them along with the relevant statistics you have gathered.

If your position, finally, is abolished, it is not the end of the world. Just be thankful that you are so well educated in just the work area that is growing in the present economy: information handling and use, communication. You can, of course, look for another job in a school library media center, or in a public or academic library, but you may want to explore bringing your expertise to another setting, a business or other agency. Special librarianship is the fastest-growing part of the profession; perhaps with some additional training you can use your skills to organize library and information services in some innovative and pioneering way.

You can, if you set your mind and spirit to it, emerge from the stress of job loss and job change with more confidence and more proficiency in organizing yourself to manage and produce, and freer from destructive stress than you have ever been before.

Stress-Creating Situation

You have just received word that your media aide will be eliminated the following year. She is essential to the full implementation of your library media program. You are very upset and develop severe migraine headaches.

Stress-Reduction Response

After considering any side effects, which of the following would you choose as the most effective alternative?

1. You complain to the principal and write a letter of protest to the superintendent.
2. You ask the Parent-Teacher Association president to work with you on identifying a group of parent volunteers to assume some of the aide's duties.
3. At a PTA meeting you present a program illustrated with slides on the library media program

with emphasis on the contributions of the library media aide.
4. You ask the district library media consultant and the state library media supervisor to intervene for you.
5. You assemble the following data you have been accumulating ever since you heard at a meeting of the Board of Trustees that there was a possibility of a decrease in financial support:
    A job description of the library media aide.
    The number of teachers and students who have benefited from the aide's activities.
    The increase in the library media center's holdings.
    A list of the ways the library media program has expanded and the increased associated duties.
    A comparison of the spot-check on circulation before and after the aide was employed.
    A petition in favor of the aide's position signed by the teachers.
    You present all this information to the principal and to the superintendent and ask permission to present it to the Board of Education.

Summary of Stress-Survival Strategies

Internal

> Develop a flexible attitude toward your work and toward your established practices and program.
> Maintain a realistic view of your own behavior. Honestly accept your weaknesses and your strengths. Learn to like yourself.
> Become proficient in self-relaxing skills and practice them often.
> Be accessible to others and open to their ideas and suggestions.
> Take an impersonal attitude in interpersonal relations. If you take everything personally you're in trouble.
> Demonstrate your enjoyment of your work and your pleasure in working with others.

External

> Make a detailed plan for action in response to a stressful situation.
> Identify and associate with a supportive person with whom you can discuss your concerns.

- Become skillful in communicating and make a practice of communicating often with others in the school community.
- Give other faculty members the understanding and respect they deserve as professionals and human beings. Build their self-esteem.
- Develop a warm, caring relationship with students, showing them that you are interested in them and want to help with their learning problems.
- Be sure that everyone understands your role in the school program and in community relations.
- Participate in the planning for a proposed change and become a force for its success.
- Read, study and become informed about any proposed change.
- Follow a planned program of professional growth to increase your professional expertise and credibility.
- Join with others in the education and library professions to organize lobbying groups to inform government office seekers and incumbents about the crucial need for expanded efforts for a higher quality of education and libraries.

Appendix A

Relaxation Therapy

Two general approaches to therapeutic relaxation

Relaxing the mind:
1. Understand the mechanism of your tension.
2. See your problems and yourself in perspective.
3. Realize that anger and impatience retard rather than facilitate your plans.
4. Cultivate an attitude of self-tolerance.
5. Substitute reasonable planning for emotional demanding.

Relaxing the muscles:
1. Become aware of the feelings involved in muscular tension by deliberately contracting one muscle group at a time, starting with the large muscles.
2. "Talk to" the various muscle groups, telling them to "let go, let go" more and more. Repeat this once or twice a day.
3. Practice "differential relaxation," that is, reduce contraction of muscles directly employed in an action and at the same time relax the muscles not involved, such as relaxing the left arm while writing with the right.

From *The Encyclopedia of Human Behavior*, vol. 2, Garden City: Doubleday and Company, Inc., 1970.

Appendix B

Test on Principal/Library Media Specialist Relationships

(Mark each statement + or -)

1. ( ) The principal leaves the development of the library media program to the library media specialist.
2. ( ) The library media specialist invites the principal to visit the media center frequently.
3. ( ) The principal is always too busy to talk with the library media specialist.
4. ( ) The principal has an inflexible attitude about the ways the media center is used.
5. ( ) The principal offers constructive suggestions for the library media program.
6. ( ) The library media specialist keeps the principal informed about trends and innovations in the school library media field.
7. ( ) The principal believes it is important to schedule conferences with the library media specialist periodically.
8. ( ) The library media specialist and the principal have different philosophies about the media center program and operation.
9. ( ) The principal is interested in participating in planning the objectives of the library media program.

10. ( ) The library media specialist talks with the principal only when a problem arises.
11. ( ) The principal thinks the library media specialist should be involved in curriculum planning.
12. ( ) The principal never shows his/her appreciation of the library media specialist's efforts.
13. ( ) The principal encourages creative uses of the resources of the library media center.
14. ( ) The library media specialist shows a lack of understanding of the principal's responsibilities.
15. ( ) The principal supports the library media specialist in the implementation of the materials selection policy.
16. ( ) The principal shows concern for the welfare of the library media specialist.
17. ( ) The library media specialist seeks the principal's cooperation in the development of procedures evaluating the media program.
18. ( ) The principal files the library media program reports without discussing and reviewing them with the library media specialist.
19. ( ) The principal and library media specialist disagree about the latter's job description.
20. ( ) The principal supports and promotes the library media program.

Plus answers denote a good relationship.
Give 5 points for each plus answer.
Top possible score — 55.

1. −	11. +
2. +	12. −
3. −	13. +
4. −	14. −
5. +	15. +
6. +	16. +
7. +	17. +
8. −	18. −
9. +	19. −
10. −	20. +

APPENDIX C

CHART OF CHILD NEEDS

NEEDS	FROM PARENTS	FROM EDUCATORS	FROM PLAYMATES	FROM COMMUNITY
EMOTIONAL *Affection* (feeling of being loved)	Comradeship. Playing no favorites. Serenity in home.	Evident fondness for child. Happy cooperative atmosphere in classroom. Kindness, fairness.	Friendships. Interest in childs' achievements.	Understanding teachers. Active child welfare agencies and kind foster parents when home supervision breaks down.
Belonging (feeling of being wanted by the group)	Significant share in family work and play. Proud of child as member of family.	Welcoming child in school and giving real share in activities of classroom and playground.	Full acceptance of child. Genuine share in group's activities.	Inspiring child's cooperation to contribute to the beauty, health and welfare of community.
Independence (feeling of managing and directing own life)	Child helped to stand on own feet. Given opportunities to make decisions and choose friends with reasonable guidance.	Initiative encouraged. Participation in class discussions. Training in self control and self direction.	Child given his turn in doing things and being leader.	Opportunities for older children and youth to participate in community councils.
Achievement (satisfaction from making things and doing jobs)	Encouragement in school work. Opportunities for worthwhile tasks; hobbies and adventure.	Work at which child can succeed. Opportunities for success in sports; hobbies; dramatics, etc.	Child included in school projects, sports, dramatics, musical and other activities.	Vocational guidance. Share in community enterprises—salvage campaigns, victory gardens, church activities, etc.

Social Approval (feeling that others approve of conduct and effort)	Praise for good behavior, honest effort in work and other accomplishments (sports, making friends, etc.)	Commendation for good behavior, diligence in school work, success in sports, dramatics, music, dramatics, etc.	Generous admiration for child's accomplishments in school work, sports, dramatics, etc.	Credit for constructive activities, patriotic work, etc.
Self Esteem (feeling of being worthwhile)	Confidence in child and his future.	Making child feel a worthwhile person. Helping child understand and accept himself.	Appreciation of child's good qualities.	Making child feel he matters to community. Giving him share in community enterprises.
CHARACTER AND SOCIAL (for developing ability to live with others in cooperative and worthy way)	Good patterns of behavior at home, encouraging honesty, sincerity, social service, and spiritual development. Sex education.	Training child to cooperate with others in work and play and to complete difficult tasks for worthwhile ends.	Approval of child when a good sport (poor loser, good winner, etc.)	Good character-building agencies—schools, churches, playgrounds, day nurseries, recreation centers, etc.
INTELLECTUAL (for training in ability to think clearly and solve problems wisely)	Encouraging children to find out the facts before coming to conclusions.	Training children to think in an orderly fashion, to acquire sound study habits, and to read widely.	Participation in group projects planned and carried out by children themselves.	Compulsory education. Inviting partnership of children in helping solve community problems. Developing partnership between home and school.
PHYSICAL (for developing a healthy body and good health habits)	Nutritious food, adequate sleep, suitable clothing, sanitary living quarters, medical and dental care, training in good health habits, outdoor activities.	Health education, physical training, cooperation with medical authorities in health inspection and immunization against disease.	Consideration by child of health and handicaps of associates. Full cooperation in preventing spread of contagious diseases.	Adequate medical and dental services. Immunization against diseases. Sanitary living conditions. Full social security.

Prepared by the National Committee of Mental Hygiene (now Health and Welfare Canada) for the Canadian Broadcasting Corporation. © 1981 Canadian Broadcasting Corporation Quoted by permission

Appendix D

Volunteer Program*

The board encourages the use of community resources and citizens to assist in furthering the educational program.

Volunteer Program

Citizen interest and involvement in the education of children can be a meaningful part of the school program. The use of constructive volunteer services will improve the quality of education for all children. Effective volunteer services can:

1. Help improve academic achievement in children by allowing teachers and other school staff more time for professional instruction;
2. Extend services to school children through the use of volunteers from each school community;
3. Provide resources from the community for enrichment of the school program;
4. Increase community understanding of the problems facing public schools and enlist the support of citizens in an effort to improve education; and,
5. Provide an exchange of ideas, concerns, and proposals between school personnel and citizens of the community.

Volunteers shall be encouraged to perform tasks which enrich and supplement the everyday school program. Their services are utilized to make it possible for the professional to use his skill and training more effectively. Volunteers shall work under the supervision of the principal and direction of the area coordinator of volunteers. The director of staff communications shall give assistance as needed to provide district-wide consistency. It shall be the responsibility of the school staff to determine the limits and scope of volunteer activities. Volunteers shall be encouraged to make recommendations concerning their function.

In order to ensure protection of students, staff and volunteers, a proficient method of implementation of the volunteer program will be followed. Handbooks will be furnished to all school principals to include guidelines for the following phases of the volunteer program:

1. Identification of school needs;
2. Appointment of school volunteer chairman;
3. Recruitment of volunteers;
4. Arrangements for volunteer orientations;
5. Screening and assignment of volunteers;
6. Training of volunteers;
7. Supervision of volunteers;
8. Reporting periodically;
9. Recognition of volunteer services; and,
10. Evaluation of the program.

Ethics for Volunteers

My interest and concern for children and my belief that better education provides for more meaningful living has challenged me to become a part of the effort to improve and enrich the educational experiences offered by the School District of Greenville County.

I understand that I, as a volunteer, do not replace a teacher, but that I offer supplementary services which can increase a teacher's effectiveness.

I recognize that a professional will decide the duties I will perform, the authority I will be given and the information and materials I will need. I will accept responsibilities as assigned and will expect to account for these services.

I realize that love and respect for children are the most important ingredients in working effectively with them. I value the achievements of children, enjoy working with them, and will keep confidential information about them confidential.

I will contribute to the success of the over-all volunteer program by being dependable and consistent, by following regulations and procedures, by discussing specific problems with the volunteer coordinator, and by observing discretion in commenting on school matters.

*Quoted with permission from the *Board Policy Manual* of the School District of Greenville County, S.C.

Appendix E

*Materials Selection Policy

The board delegates to professional personnel the authority for the selection of materials in their respective areas. Professional employees involved in procuring or developing instructional materials should seek to

1. Provide materials that will enrich and support the curriculum, taking into consideration the varied interests, abilities, and maturity levels of the pupils served;
2. Provide materials that will stimulate the growth in critical thinking that leads to the development of concepts, broad understandings, literary appreciation, aesthetic values, and ethical standards;
3. Provide a background of information which will enable pupils to make intelligent decisions for appropriate behavior in changing situations;
4. Provide materials on opposing sides of controversial issues so that young citizens may develop under guidance the practice of critical reading and thinking;
5. Provide materials representative of the many religious, ethnic, and cultural groups and their contributions to our society;
6. Provide materials having the positive values of respect for human dignity and of insight into many cultural patterns; and,

7. Provide materials which will develop in children an appreciation of their nation's heritage, of their own responsibilities as citizens in a world of democracy, and of their country's contribution to world progress.

The superintendent shall designate the steps in a routine procedure for handling materials that may be questioned by individuals or groups within the community.

All instructional materials, books, (including texts, library, or supplementary) and equipment will be selected in accord with the following procedures and guidelines:

I. Although the principal shall be responsible for the implementation of these procedures and the use of these guidelines in the selection of instructional materials, books, and equipment, teachers, librarians, resource personnel, and consultants will participate extensively in the evaluation and selection process. All textbooks and supplementary textbooks shall be evaluated according to the criteria.

II. Using these administrative guidelines and other board approved policies, professional personnel select materials based on the following needs:
   A. Needs of the individual school:
      a. Based on the knowledge of curriculum,
      b. Based on requests from administrators and teachers;
   B. Needs of the individual student:
      a. Based on knowledge of children and youth,
      b. Based on requests of parents and students;
   C. Provision of a wide range of materials on all levels of difficulty, with a diversity of appeal and the presentation of different points of view;
   D. Provision of materials of high artistic quality; and,
   E. Provision of materials with superior format.
   ALL MATERIALS MUST BE EITHER LISTED ON APPROVED LISTS OR EXAMINED PERSONALLY BY PROFESSIONAL PERSONNEL BEFORE PURCHASE.

III. In selecting materials in sensitive areas or on controversial issues, teachers, librarians, and administrators should consider the following:

A. Religion—Factual, unbiased materials on all major religions should be available for student use.
B. Ideologies—Students should have access to basic factual information, suitable to their maturity level, on any either favorable or unfavorable, in government, current events, politics, education, or any other phase of life.
C. Sex, profanity, and obscenity—Professional personnel should subject materials of this type to a stern test of literary merit and reality. The District would not in any case endorse obscenity, salacious profanity, or graphic sexual incidents. The fact, however, that sexuality or expressive language do appear in recognized materials should not automatically disqualify them. Rather the decision should be based on whether the materials present life in true proportions, whether circumstances are realistically dealt with, and whether literary values are present. At all times, consideration must be given to the maturity level of the student.
D. Science—To be truly educated scientifically, students should have opportunities to examine scientific research and theories and should be encouraged to arrive at their own logical conclusions, based on the scientific process. Emphasis should be placed upon the theoretical nature of some of the subjects.

IV. SELECTION OF BOOKS NOT ON STATE APPROVED LISTS—In order to insure group participation in the selection process of books which are not on state approved lists, a district book selection committee will be appointed by the superintendent, to be composed of administrators and teachers. This committee will insure that all books *not on state approved lists* have been selected in accordance with the criteria lists above and that these procedures and guidelines are strictly adhered to throughout the district.
   A. Before purchase and/or use in the schools, lists of books will be submitted to the books selection committee with the process of selection outlined on the request.

B. The committee will not approve the selection of books by individuals or those not in accord with the procedures detailed above.
V. If a student and/or his parents object to non-textbook materials because of moral or ethical reasons, he should be given additional alternatives or choices.

Controversial Issues

The unique contribution of the study of controversial affairs is two-fold: it brings a sense of dedication to the total democratic way as well as proficiency in those means by which mankind can approach more closely full democracy. The freedom to teach controversial issues is, therefore, a responsibility of all teachers; and it is believed that an unbiased and objective discussion of controversial issues is necessary in a free and healthy system of learning.

Courses of study should include those issues which are relevant to the course, meaningful to the student, and consistent with concerns expressed by the student.

Students should be encouraged to acquire such democratic attitudes as the following:

1. To respect the opinions of others;
2. To maintain a sense of responsibility in regard to working with those who hold different opinions;
3. To think critically and to be open-minded;
4. To reach decisions based on consideration of facts;
5. To seek new facts and to accept new evidence; and,
6. To reserve judgment until the full issue is presented.

As citizens, teachers have the right to personal opinions on controversial subjects; they also have the professional responsibility to refrain from expressing their personal opinions in group discussion. It is the teacher's role to facilitate discussion by seeing that all facts, evidence, and aspects of an issue are honestly presented and that students are helped to evaluate their sources of data as well as their own procedures and conclusions.

To implement the board policy dealing with this topic, personnel should observe the following administrative and teaching regulations.

For principals:
1. Assign only teachers of superior training and experience to teach subjects where the discussion of controversial topics occurs most often;
2. Remind teachers that they do not *teach* controversial issues, but rather provide opportunities for their *study*.

For Teachers:
1. Deal with controversial topics as impartially and objectively as possible. Do not intrude personal biases;
2. Handle all such topics in a manner suited to the range of knowledge, maturity, and competence of the students;
3. Have teaching materials dealing with all possible aspects of the topics readily available;
4. Don't manufacture an issue. Take up only those that are current and real. When you do, you will be able to find up-to-date teaching materials in the current press and periodical literature. Generally your best single sources of reliable information will come from those places, plus court decisions and legal opinions;
5. Do not expect or require that the class reach an agreement;
6. Whenever in doubt about the advisability of taking up a given "hot" topic, consult the principal; and,
7. Remember that the policy of the board is designed to protect you as well as your pupils from unfair or inconsiderate criticism whenever your pupils are studying a controversial subject.

COMPLAINTS

Questions or Challenges on Books and Materials

If a student objects to or finds any materials offensive, he should be given additional alternatives or choices. Any parent or citizen, also, has a right to lodge a complaint against any reading material being used in the school system. If the complaint cannot be resolved satisfactorily during a conference with the prinicipal and the teacher concerned, then the following procedure should be used.

1. A complaint shall be filed by completing the form entitled "Citizen's Request for Reconsideration of a Book." (Forms are available in all schools, area offices, and at the district office);
2. The complaint shall be submitted to the appropriate area assistant superintendent;
3. The complaint will be submitted to the district Materials Review Committee by the area assistant superintendent;
4. The committee will examine the books or materials in question and evaluate them in relation to the needs of the curriculum and to the needs and interests of the readers for whom they were purchased; and,
5. The committee will provide summaries of the evaluation as information for area assistant superintendents, principals, librarians, teachers, students, and citizens.

*Quoted with permission from the *Board Policy Manual* of the School District of Greenville County, S.C.

Citizen's Request for Reconsideration of a Book

Author _____ Hardcover   Paperback
Title
Publisher (If known)
Request initiated by _____
Telephone _____ Address _____
City _____ Zone _____
Complainant represents
_____ himself
_____ (Name organization) _____
_____ (Identify other group) _____
1. To what in the book do you object? (Please be specific; cite pages

2. What do you feel might be the result of reading this book?

3. For what age group would you recommend this book? _____
4. Is there anything good about this book? _____
5. Did you read the entire book? _____ What parts? _____
7. Are you aware of the judgment of this book by literary critics?

7. What do you believe is the theme of this book? _____

8. What would you like your school to do about this book?
_____ do not assign it to my child
_____ withdraw it from all students as well
            as from my child
_____ send it to the County Book Evaluation
       Committee for reevaluation
9. In its place what book of equal literary quality would you recommend that would convey as valuable a picture and perspective of our civilization?
_____
_____

Signature of Complainant _____

APPENDIX F

EVALUATIONS OF COMPUTER SOFTWARE

There is a mountain of software information available for educators. The following source list, arranged in alphabetical order, is the result of sifting through a portion of the existing data.

1983 Classroom Computer News Directory of Educational Computing Resources, basic sourcebook published by Intentional Educations, 341 Mt. Auburn Street, Watertown, Mass. 02172, $14.95.

Courseware Report Card, 150 West Carob Street, Compton, Calif. 90220. Two editions (elementary and secondary) appear five times annually, $49.95.

EPIE & Consumers Union, PO Box 620, Stony Brook, N.Y. 11790. $75-$300.

The International Council for Computers in Education (ICCE), Department of Computer and Information Science, University of Oregon, Eugene, Ore. 97403. Largest nonprofit computer-educators organization; individual membership $16.50. Membership includes subscription to the Computing Teacher.

Microcomputer Directory: Applications in Educational Settings, available from Monroe C. Gutman Library, Appian Way, Cambridge, Mass. 02138, $15. A guide to computer projects nationwide.

Microcomputer Software and Information for Teachers, Northwest Regional Education Laboratory, 300 Southwest Sixth Avenue, Portland, Ore. 97204. Software reviews in published form or through on-line data base with average cost of $4 to $5 a search. To access Resources in Computer Education (RICE) data base, school agency or organization must be a subscriber to Bibliographic Retrieval Services Inc. (BRS). If not already a BRS subscriber, one-time $150 membership fee is required to join the School Practices Information Network, which automatically makes one a subscriber to BRS. Application available from BRS Inc., 1200 Route 7, Latham, N.Y. 12110.

Minnesota Educational Computer Consortium, 2520 Broadway Drive, Saint Paul, Minn. 55113. Free catalogue of Apple and Atari Software.

Resource Handbook, basic sourcebook by Technical Education Research Centers, 8 Eliot Street, Cambridge, Mass. 02168, $10 plus $2 for shipping.

School Microware Reviews appears three times yearly from Dresden Associates, PO Box 246, Dresden, Maine 04342. One-year subscription, $45.

SOFTSWAP, Microcomputer Center at the San Mateo County Office of Education, 333 Main Street, Redwood City, Calif. 94063. Has library of more than 300 public-domain programs that are free to educators who bring their own disks to the center. Will swap copy of any program in its noncommercial library for original software contribution from an educator. Sells disks (with from five to 30 programs per disk) for $10.

Special Education Computer Technology Online Resource (SECTOR Project) of Exceptional Children, UMC68, Utah State University, Logan, Utah. Send self-addressed envelope for evaluation from or list of companies that offer preview copies.

From *The Christian Science Monitor*, April 15, 1983

Sources of Computer Software Reviews

Purser's Magazine, P.O. Box 466, El Dorado, CA 95623
MACUL, 33500 Van Born Road, Wayne, MI 48184

Journal of Courseware Review (Apple only), Apple Foundation, 20863 Stevens Creek Blvd., Building B-2, Suite A-I, Cupertina, CA 95014

InfoWorld, 530 Lytton, Palo Alto, CA 94301

Creative Computing, P.O. Box 789-M, Morristown, NJ 07960

Personal Computing, P.O. Box 1408, Riverton, NJ 08077

Nibble (Apple only), P.O. Box 325, Lincoln, MA 01773

Pipeline CONDUIT, P.O. Box 388, Iowa City, IA 52244

Popular Computing, P.O. Box 307, Martinsville, NJ 08836

Queue, 5 Chapel Hill, Fairfield, CT 06432

The Computing Teacher, Dept. of Computer and Information Science, University of Oregon, Eugene, OR 97403

Classroom Computer News, P.O. Box 266, Cambridge, MA 02138

Byte, P.O. Box 590, Martinsville, NJ 08836

Electronic Learning, 902 Sylvan Ave., Englewood Cliffs, NJ 07632

School Microware, Dresden Association, Box 246, Dresden, ME 04342

(This list appeared in the May/June 1982 issue of the *News Bulletin of ComputerTown USA!*)

APPENDIX G

INFORMATION FOR THE MENTALLY AND PHYSICALLY HANDICAPPED AND THE CULTURALLY AND ETHNICALLY DIFFERENT

Materials for the Handicapped

Coordinating Council for Handicapped Children
    407 South Dearborn St., Room 680, Chicago, IL 60605
Center for Rehabilitation Information,
    Library of Health Sciences
    201 Medical Sciences Building, University of Illinois, Urbana, IL 61801
Ray Graham Association for the Handicapped
    Administrative Offices, 970 North Oaklawn Avenue, Elmhurst, IL 60126
National Association of the Physically Handicapped
    Grandville Avenue, Detroit, MI 48228
Division for the Blind and Physically Handicapped
    Library of Congress, Washington, D.C. 20542
National Association of Parents of the Blind-Deaf
    525 Opus Avenue, Capitol Heights, MD 20027
National Braille Book Bank
    85 Goodwin Avenue, Midland Park, NJ 07432
American Foundation for the Blind
    15 West 16th Street, New York, NY 10011
Keith Jennison Books/Franklin Watts, Inc. (Large-print books)

845 Third Avenue, New York, NY 10022
Captioned Films for the Deaf
  Distribution center, 5034 Wisconsin Avenue, N.W., Washington, D.C. 20016
National Association of the Deaf
  814 Thayer Avenue, Silver Spring, MD 20910
American Association on Mental Deficiency
  5201 Connecticut Avenue, N.W., Washington, D.C. 30015
Association for Children with Learning Disabilities
  99 Park Ave. 6th Floor, New York, N.Y. 10016
National Association for Retarded Citizens
  P.O. Box 6109, 2709 Avenue E, East, Arlington, TX 76011
National Association for Mental Health
  1800 North Kent St., Rosslyn, VA 22209
United Cerebral Palsy Association
  66 East 34th Street, New York, NY 10016
Muscular Dystrophy Association of America
  1790 Broadway, New York, NY 10019

Materials for the Culturally and Ethnically Different

Black Child Development Institute
  1463 Rhode Island Avenue, N.W., Washington, D.C. 20005
Black Resources Information Coordinating Services
  P.O. Box 6353, Tallahassee, FL 32304
Ethnic Materials Information Exchange Task Force
  68-71 Bell Blvd., Bayside, NY 11364
National Association of Interdisciplinary Ethnic Studies
  Ethnic Studies Department, California State Polytechnic University, Pomona, CA 91768

Appendix H

Planning Curriculum Units

Teacher/Library Media Specialist Collaboration

They develop objectives for the unit.
They specify the topics and concepts to be introduced and reinforced.
They identify special student needs, interests, goals, abilities.
They list the media skills which must be mastered and indicate the appropriate times for the skills to be taught as they are needed.
They identify a broad range of materials indicating the concepts and the ability levels for which they are suited.
They devise learning experiences to implement the objectives. They may include any of the following:
    Field trips to community sites.
    Presentations by community members.
    Student productions of slide-tape sequences, transparency sets, video-tapes, 8mm films, 35mm still pictures, filmstrips.
    Individualized learning packages.
    Independent study.
    Simulation.
    Role playing.
    Use of learning centers.
    Oral history projects.

Use of a microcomputer.
Original drama presentations.
Preparation of models, displays.
Use of games.
Tape-recording of interviews of community members.

They specify various modes of using certain media for planned purposes—whole class, small groups, individual students.

They plan the production of instructional materials and decide who will be responsible for the work. Any of the following might be selected:

Non-print materials	Pretests
Flash cards	Charts and posters
Work sheets	Activity cards
Stencils	Learning centers
Learning packages	Games
Crossword puzzles	Simulations
Flannel-board story characters	

They discuss appropriate evaluation procedures for each objective.

They develop the following chart:

| *Objectives* | *Materials With Indicated Ability Levels* | *Media Skills Needed* | *Student Activities** | *Evaluation* |

*I — Individual
 S — Small group
 C — Whole class

(The teacher and the library media specialist will fill in this chart according to the unit they are working on).

APPENDIX I

GUIDELINES FOR GROUP LEADERSHIP

Primary Purpose of the Leader
To guide discussion along its course from analysis to decision. To help the group realize its fullest potentialities in the thinking process.

Suggestions for Effective Leadership
1. Inform yourself about the subject to be discussed.
2. Know your group, their needs, abilities, and expectations.
3. Know what is expected of you as a leader. Stimulator? Coordinator? Mediator? Degree of formality?
4. Plan the discussion. Sample outline:
    I. Analysis of question or problem: extent, importance, causes, etc.
    II. Desirable goals in this area.
    III. Possible solutions or decisions and selection of preferred solution.
    IV. Methods of achieving preferred solution.
    V. Conclusion
5. Distribute any available resource material to group members. Arrange for resource people to be present at discussion.
6. Provide for physical comfort of group.
    Arrange for comfortable light, ventilation, and temperature.

Seat members in circle or semi-circle if possible.
Eliminate distractions.
7. Open the discussion with brief introduction.
   Focus group's attention on subject, pointing out importance, timeliness, pertinence, etc.
   Define terms.
   Clarify purpose of discussion.
8. Promote progressive development of group thinking.
   Refrain from imposing your ideas upon the group.
   Try to have all of the important facts brought out.
   Call attention to points of agreement.
   Draw attention away from irrelevant issues by means of questions or summaries.
   Limit discussion of issues on which it is plain no agreement can be reached.
   Summarize and interpret discussion at various times.
   Instead of answering questions directed to you, refer them to the group.
   Use stimulating questions to move discussion along.
   Have significant points recorded on chalkboard.
9. Promote evenness of participation.
   Keep all contributions short. Break in with minor summaries and comments.
   Accept each contribution as worthy of thought.
   Encourage the non-contributor with a nod or word, a request for his opinion, or a question which can be answered yes or no.
10. Prevent confusion, unnecessary disagreement and antagonism.
    Clarify or ask for clarification of vague terms.
    Intervene in cases of misinterpretation or misunderstanding.
11. Close the discussion, or appoint a participant to do this.
    Summarize discussion points.
    Reveal extent of agreement or disagreement.
    State any solutions, or plans of action decided upon.
    Give participants opportunity to confirm this summary.

Bibliography

1. Aaron, Shirley L. "Teaming for Learning." *School Media Quarterly* 4:215-18, Spring 1976.
2. Abrego, Phil, and Brammer, Lawrence. *Developing Coping Skills for Career Related Changes.* Palo Alto, Cal.: American Institutes for Research in the Behaviorial Sciences, 1979.
3. Albert, Ellis. "What People Can Do for Themselves to Cope with Stress," in *Stress at Work*, edited by Cary L. Cooper and Roy Payne. Chichester: John Wiley and Sons, 1978.
4. Anderson, Robert A. *Stress Power: How to Turn Tension into Energy.* New York: Human Sciences Press, 1978.
5. Angelotti, Michael. "Plug into TV Now." *School Library Journal* 27:49, September 1980.
6. Antonovsky, Aaron. *Health, Stress, and Coping.* San Francisco: Jossey-Bass Publishers, 1980.
7. Asheim, Lester, Baker, D. Philip, and Mathews, Virginia H. *Reading and Successful Living: The Family-School Partnership.* Hamden, Conn.: Library Professional Publications, 1983.
8. Association for Supervision and Curriculum Development. *Education for an Open Society.* Washington, D.C.: The Association, 1974.
9. Baker, D. Philip. "The School Library Media Program and the Community," in *Excellence in School Media Pro-*

grams, edited by Thomas J. Galvin et al. Chicago: American Library Association, 1980.
10. Baker, D. Philip, and Bender, David R. *Library Media Programs and the Special Learner.* Hamden, Conn.: Library Professional Publications, 1981.
11. Bardo, Pamela. "The Pain of Teacher Burnout: A Case History." *Phi Delta Kappan* 61:252-53, December 1979.
12. Barnes, Ronald E. "An Educator Looks Back from 1996." *the Futurist* 12:123-26, April 1976.
13. Barron, Daniel. "Role of the Media Program and Specialist in Community Education." *School Media Quarterly* 7:12-17, Fall 1978.
14. Baskin, Barbara H. and Karen H. "Gifted Children and the Elementary School Librarian—Theory into Practice," in *The Special Child in the Library.* Chicago: American Library Association, 1976.
15. Bateman, Thomas. "Work Overload." *Business Horizons* 24:23-27, September-October, 1981.
16. Batt, Doris. "The Hearing Impaired Child in the Library," in *The Special Child in the Library.* Chiciago: American Library, 1976.
17. Benson, Charles S. "Financial Alternatives for Urban School Districts." *Phi Delta Kappan* 63:530-33, April 1982.
18. Benton, Robert D. "Technology and the Fox Fire Syndrome: A Prospective." *School Library Media Quarterly* 10:30-37, Fall 1981.
19. Besant, Jane. "You can Woo and Winn Teachers." *Wisconsin Library Bulletin* 73:146-48, July 1977.
20. Bold, Rudolph. "Librarian Burn-Out." *Library Journal,* Nov. 1, 1982.
21. Bonn, Geore S., and Faibisoff, Sylvia. *Changing Times: Changing Libraries.* Urbana-Champaign: University of Illinois, 1976.
22. Breed, Patricia. "Being a Squeaky Wheel." *Illinois Libraries,* September 1978.
23. Brown, Arnold. "Equipping Ourselves for the Communications Age." *The Futurist* 15:53-57, August 1981.
24. Buchen, Irving H. *Curriculum 2000: Future Basics.* Washington, D.C.: U.S. Department of Health, Education and Welfare, 1980.

25. Bunstead, Richard A. "Our Massachusetts School System Adapts to Proposition 2-1/2." *Phi Delta Kappan* 62:722-25, June 1981.
26. "Coping With Anxiety at AT&T." *Business Week* 79:95+, May 28, 1979.
27. Byrne, Richard B. "As Through a Glass Darkly; Planning for the Unknowable Media Future." *School Library Media Quarterly* 10:22-28, Fall 1981.
28. Casciano-Savignano, C. Jennie. "Interpersonal Relationships in Secondary Schools." *NASSP Bulletin* 60:26-30.
29. "Challenges of the Eighties: Exciting Times in Science and Technology." *U.S. News and World Report* 87:73-74, Oct. 15, 1979.
30. "Challenges of the Eighties: Whatever You Want, A School Will Teach It." *U.S. News and World Report* 87:73-74, Oct. 15, 1979.
31. Cheatham, Bertha M. "On to the Year 2000: Libraries in 1981." *School Library Media Quarterly* 28:15-19, December 1981.
32. Clatworthy, F. James. "Designing Educational Futures." Paper presented at the World Future Society Education Section, Houston, Texas, 1978.
33. Colberg, Donald, and Blake, Dorothy. "Another Option— The Alternative School." *Wilson Library Bulletin* 50:381-85, January 1976.
34. Combs, Arthur W. "What the Future Demands of Education." *Phi Delta Kappan* 62:369-72, January 1981.
35. Cornish, Blake M. "The Smart Machines of Tomorrow: Implications for Society." *The Futurist* 15:5-13, August 1981.
36. Cornish, Edward. "The Coming of an Information Society." *The Futurist* 15:14-21, April 1981.
37. Costa, Betty. "Microcomputer in Colorado—It's Elementary!" *Wilson Library Bulletin* 55:676-78, May 1981.
38. Cowan, Robert C. "Study: Computerized Information Will Remold Society." *Christian Science Monitor* Oct. 29, 1981.
39. Daniel, Evelyn H. "Professionalism of School Librarian and Media Center Management," in *Excellence in School Media Programs,* edited by Thomas J. Galvin et al. Chicago: American Library Association, 1980.

40. Deane, Stuart. "The Cash Crunch in the Classroom." *Today's Education* 71:41, April-May, 1982.
41. Eastman, Sarah Clarke. "I'm about to be Fired; One Librarian's Tale of Frustration." *American Libraries* 10:116-17, March 1979.
42. Elder, Jenelle. "Spanish in the Media Center." *Wisconsin Library Bulletin* 74:223-24, September-October, 1978.
43. Ely, Donald P. "Creating the Conditions for Change," in *Changing Times: Changing Libraries* by George S. Bonn and Sylvia Faibisoff, Urbana-Champaign: University of Illinois, 1976.
44. Fast, Betty. "Media and the Handicapped Child," in *Excellence in School Media Programs*, edited by Thomas J. Galvin et al. Chicago: American Library Association, 1980.
45. Fast, Betty. "The Media Specialist as an Agent for Change," in *Excellence in School Media Programs*, edited by Thomas J. Galvin et al. Chicago: American Library Association, 1980.
46. Fisher, B. Aubrey. *Small Group Decision-making: Communication and the Group Process.* New York: McGraw-Hill, 1974.
47. Fitzgibbons, Shirley A. "Professionalism and Ethical Behavior: Relationship to School Media Personnel." *School Media Quarterly* 8:82-100+, Winter 1980.
48. Fizzell, Robert L. *An Educational Model for the Future.* A paper presented to the Education Section of the World Future Society, Houston, Texas, 1978.
49. Freel, Judy. "Is There a Media Specialist in the House?" *Learning Today* 8:54-59, Fall 1975.
50. Fuhrman, Susan. "School Finance Reform in the 1980's." *Educational Leadership* 38:122-24, November 1980.
51. Galloway, Charles M. "Interpersonal Relations and Education." *Education Digest* 42:42-44, May 1977.
52. Gazda, George M., et al. *Human Relations Development: A Manual for Educators.* Boston: Allyn and Bacon, 1973.
53. Georgiades, William, et al. *New Schools for a New Age.* Santa Monica: Goodyear Publishing Company, 1977.
54. Girard, Kathryn Lee. "How to Avoid Conflict When You Can—How to Confront It When You Have To." *Ms* 7:49+, October 1978.

55. Gleaves, Edwin S. "The School Media Center: the Changing Scene." *Peabody Journal of Education* 55:169-204, April 1978.
56. Grazier, Margaret Hayes. "A Role for Media Specialists in the Curriculum Development Process." *School Media Quarterly* 4:179-204, Spring 1976.
57. Grazier, Margaret Hayes. "the Curriculum Consultant Role of the School Media Specialist." *Library Trends* 28:263-79, Fall 1979.
58. Greenberger, Robert S. "How Burn-out Affects Corporate Managers and Their Performance." *Wall Street Journal*, Apr. 23, 1981.
59. Griffin, Thomas. "There'll Be Some Changes Made." *Atlantic Monthly* 244:26-29, September 1979.
60. Guenther, Robert. "Stress Management Plans Abound But All Programs Are Not Run Well." *Wall Street Journal*, Sept. 30, 1982.
61. Gwitt, Carolyn. "Special Report: A Winning Role for the School Library." *Wilson Library Bulletin* 52:295-97, December 1977.
62. Hall, Sandra K. "Answering the Challenge of Teletest, Viewdata Systems and Other Fast Growing Communications, Such as Home Computers." Paper prepared at the Summer Workshop of the Arizona Newspaper Association, Flagstaff, Ariz., June 21, 1980.
63. Harris, James A. "Parents and Teachers, Inc." *Teacher* 96:85-87, September 1978.
64. Havelock, Ronald G., and Mary C. *Training for Change Agents*. Ann Arbor: University of Michigan, 1973.
65. Heller, Dawn H. "So What about Networks?" *School Library Journal* 25:38, December 1978.
66. Heller, Dawn, and Montgomery, Ann S. "The Media Specialist between a Rock and a Hard Place." *Illinois Libraries*, September 1978.
67. Higgins, C. Wayne, and Philips, Billy U. "How Company Sponsored Fitness Programs Keep Employees on the Job." *Management Review* 68:52-55, December 1979.
68. Hodgkinson, Harold L. "What Principals Can Do to Manage Schools in the '80s." *NASSP Bulletin* 66:41-52, February 1982.
69. Hostrop, Richard W., ed. *Foundations of Futurology in*

Education. Palm Springs, Cal.: ETC Publications, 1973.
70. Hunter, Carolyn. "Planning for Change: Three Critical Elements." Arlington, Va.: National School Public Relations Association, 1978.
71. "IFC/AAP Panelists View School Censorship." *School Library Journal* 27:14-16, September 1980.
72. Infantino, Cynthis Percak, ed. "Learning about Children: The 'Prime' Patrons." *Illinois Libraries,* December 1980.
73. Jackson, William D. "Educational Media in Teaching the Deaf Child," in *The Special Child in the Library.* Chicago: American Library Association, 1976.
74. Johnson, David W. *Reaching Out: Interpersonal Effectiveness and Self-Actualization.* Englewood Cliffs, N.J.: Prentice-Hall, 1972.
75. Jones, Mary Ann, and Emanuel, Joseph. "The Stages and Recovery Steps of Teacher 'Burnout.'" *Education Digest* 46:9-11, May 1981.
76. Karmos, Joseph S., and Ann H. "Interpersonnel Communication Skills." *Journal of Teacher Education* 29:42-44, September/October, 1978.
77. Kemerer, Frank R., and Hirst, Stephanie Abraham. "School Library Censorship Comes before the Supreme Court." *Phi Delta Kappan* 63:444-47, March 1982.
78. Kirst, Michael W. "Why There's a Financial Squeeze on Schools and What to Do about It." *Learning* 10:70-72, March 1982.
79. Klontz, Mary P. "The Role of the Media Center in the Education of the Disadvantaged Children." *Southeastern Librarian* 20:158-65, Fall 1970.
80. Kroth, Roger, and Blacklock, Gweneth. "Welcome in the Parent." *School Media Quarterly* 6:246-52, Summer 1978.
81. Krucoff, Carol. "Millions Now Use 'Video-display' Computer Terminals." *Greenville News-Greenville Piedmont,* Sept. 16, 1981.
82. Kuhn, David J. "Science Education in the Year 2000." *Education Digest* 44:51-53, March 1979.
83. Kutash, Irwin L., et al. *Handbook on Stress and Anxiety.* San Francisco: Jossey-Bass Publishers, 1981.
84. Land, Phyllis. "Schools, the On-line Media Connection," in *Excellence in School Media Programs,* edited by

Thomas J. Galvin et al. Chicago: American Library Association, 1980.
85. Laughlin, Mildred. "Flexible Scheduling—A Must!" *Learning Today* 12:79-81, Summer-Fall, 1979.
86. Lazaeus, Sy. *Loud and Clear.* New York: AMACON, a division of American Management Associations, 1975.
87. Leavitt, Glenn. "Time, Money and Students with Visual Limitations," in *The Special Child in the Library.* Chicago: American Library Association, 1976.
88. Lewis, Anne. "State Funds Come with Strings Attached." *Learning* 10:70, March 1982.
89. Likness, Craig S., and Thompson, George H. "Information, Imagination, and the High School Library." *Clearing House* 52:416-18, May 1979.
90. Lippitt, Ronald, et al. *The Dyamics of Planned Change.* Chicago: Harcourt, Brace and World, 1958.
91. Long, Lynette. "Human Relations Training: Goals and Strategies." *Journal of Teacher Education* 30:29-31, November-December, 1979.
92. McCall, Morgan W., Jr., and Lombardo, Michael M., ed. *Leadership, Where Else Can We Go?* Durham, N.C.: Duke University Press, 1978.
93. McDonald, Marion. "Where Teaching is the Exploring of New Ideas." *Christian Science Monitor*, Apr. 12, 1982, p. 16.
94. McLoone, Eugene P. "The Shifting Sands of Tax Support." *American Education* 17:11-14, August-September, 1981.
95. McQuade, Walter, and Aikmon, Ann. *Stress: What It Is, What It Can Do to Your Health, How to Fight Back.* New York: E.P. Dutton and Company, 1974.
96. Mancuso, James S. "Executive Stress Management." *Personnel Administrator* 24:23-26, November 1979.
97. Martin, Betty. "Interpersonal Relations and the School Library Media Specialist." *School Library Media Quarterly,* Fall, 1982.
98. Martin, Betty, and Carson, Ben. *The Principal's Handbook on the School Library Media Center.* Hamden, Conn. Library Professional Publications, 1981.
99. Martin, Betty, and Sargent, Linda. *The Teacher's Handbook on the School Library Media Center.* Hamden,

Conn.: Library Professional Publications, 1980.
100. Matthews, Carleen. *Factors of Successful Implementation*. Portland, Ore.: Northwest Regional Educational Laboratory, 1976.
101. Metcalf, Mary Jane. "Helping Hearing Impaired Students." *School Library Journal* 25:27-29, January 1979.
102. Miller, Marilyn L. "Children's Access to Library Systems." *Library Quarterly* 51:38-53, January 1981.
103. Molitor, Graham T.T. "The Path to Post-Industrial Growth." *The Futurist* 15:23-30, April 1981.
104. Morrow, Lance. "The Burnout of Almost Everyone." *Time*, 118:84, Sept. 21, 1981.
105. Mullen, Frances, and Peterson, Miriam. "Special Education and the School Librarian," in *The Special Child in the Library*. Chicago: American Library Association, 1976.
106. Neill, S.D. "Libraries in the Year 2010." *The Futurist* 15:47-51, October 1981.
107. Newcombe, P. Judson. *Some Influences on Teachers and Teaching in 2030: Projections, Predictions, and a Scenario*. Tampa: University of South Florida, 1979.
108. Ogbu, John U. *Minority Education and Caste*. New York: Academic Press, 1978.
109. Ornstein, Allan C. "Curricular Innovations and Trends: Recent Past, Present, and Future." *Peabody Journal of Education* 59:46-53, October 1981.
110. Phillips, Gerald M., and Erickson, Eugene C. *Interpersonal Dynamics in the Small Group*. New York: Random House, 1970.
111. Pinckney, H.B. "An American Dilemma: Financing Public Education." *NASSP Bulletin* 64:68-73, November 1980.
112. Platt, John. *The New Age: Learning and Teaching in the Electronic Society*. Washington, D.C.: U.S. Department of Health, Education and Welfare; National Institute of Education, 1977.
113. Pogrow, Stanley. "Foxfire Awash in the Third Wave: Illumination or Wetness." *School Library Media Quarterly* 10:38-40+, Fall 1981.
114. Portteus, Elnora M. "A Practical Look at Media Supervision and Curriculum." *School Media Quarterly* 7:204-09,

Spring 1979.
115. Reischauer, Edwin O. *Toward the 21st Century: Education for a Changing World.* New York: Alfred A. Knopf, 1973.
116. Reisler, Raymond F. "An Education Agenda for the Eighties." *Phi Delta Kappan* 62:413-14+, February 1981.
117. Roark, Albert E. "Interpersonal Conflict Management." *Personnel and Guidance Journal* 56:400-12, March 1978.
118. Rosenberg, Marc H. "What is the School Media Specialist's Role?" *Audio Visual Instruction* 23: 12-13, February 1978.
119. Roth, Edwin. "A Child Psychologist's View." *School Library Journal* 21:68-69, March 1975.
120. Rubin, Louis, ed. *The Future of Education: Perspectives on Tomorrow's Schooling.* Philadelphia: Research for Better Schools, Inc. 1975.
121. Ryans, D.G. *Characteristics of Teachers.* Washington, D.C.: American Council on Education, 1960.
122. Sailer, Heather R., Schlacter, John, and Edwards, Mark. "Stress: Causes, Consequences, and Coping Strategies." *Personnel* 59:35-48, July-August, 1982.
123. Satir, Virginia. *Making Contact.* Millbrae, Cal.: Celestial Arts, 1976.
124. Scanlon, Robert G. "The Year 2000." *Vital Speeches of the Day* 46:727-30, September 1980.
125. Schmidt, William T. "Media Specialist." *Media and Methods* 13:22-24, October 1976.
126. "Service or Sanity? Coping with Media Center Cutbacks." *Illinois Libraries* September 1978.
127. Seyle, Hans. *Stress of Life.* New York: McGraw-Hill, 1978.
128. Shane, Harold G. "A Curriculum for the New Century." *Phi Delta Kappan* 62:351-56, January 1981.
129. Sherwood, Bruce. "Interactive Electronic Media," in *Changing Times: Changing Libraries,* edited by George S. Bon and Sylvia Faibisoff. Urbana-Champaign: University of Illinois, 1976.
130. Shostak, Arthur B. "The Coming Systems Break: Technology and Schools of the Future." *Phi Delta Kappan* 62:356-59, January 1981.

131. Smith, Robert Frederick. "A Funny Thing is Happening to the Library on its Way to the Future." *The Futurist* 12:85-91, April 1978.
132. Smith, Susan. "The Research Implications of the NCLIS Task Force Report on the Role of the School Library Media Program in Networking." *School Media Quarterly* 8:179-83, Spring, 1980.
133. Spaniol, Le Roy, and Caputo, Jennifer J. *Professional Burn-Out: A Personal Survival Kit.* Lexington, Mass.: Human Services Associates, 1979.
134. Sparks, Dennis. *The Challenge Process: A Group Problem-Solving Technique.* Livonia, Mich.: Northwest Staff Development Center, 1980 (Unpublished manuscript.)
135. Sullivan, Janet S. "Initiating Instructional Design into School Library Media Programs." *School Media Quarterly* 8:251-58, Summer 1980.
136. "Teaching the Deaf with Photography," in *The Special Child in the Library.* Chicago: American Library Association, 1976.
137. Theobald, Robert, ed. *Futures Conditional.* New York: Bobbs-Merrill, 1972.
138. Thibault, John W., et al. *Contemporary Topics in Social Psychology.* Morristown, N.J.: General Learning Press, 1976.
139. "The Third Century: Twenty-six Prominent Americans Speculate on the Educational Future." New Rochelle, N.Y.: Change Magazine Press, 1977.
140. "Toward A Troubled 21st Century," *Time Magazine*, Aug. 4, 1980. p. 54.
141. Traub, James. "Futurology: The Rise of the Predicting Profession." *Saturday Review* 6:24-32, December 1979.
142. Tuttle, Dean W. "A Comparison of Three Reading Media for the Blind," in *The Special Child in the Library.* Chicago: American Library Association, 1976.
143. Tydeman, John. "Videotext: Ushering in the Electronic Household." *The Futurist* 16:54-61, February 1982.
144. Vandergrift, Kay E. "Selection: Reexamination and Reassessment." *School Media Quarterly* 6:103-111, Winter 1978.

145. Walschal, Peter H., ed. *Learning Tomorrows: Commentaries on the Future of Education.* New York: Praeger, 1979.
146. Walsh, Debbie. "Classroom Stress and Teacher Burnout." *Phi Delta Kappan* 61:253, December 1979.
147. Walson, Jerry J., and Snider, Bill C. "Book Selection Pressure on School Library Media Specialists and Teachers." *School Library Media Quarterly,* Winter 1981.
148. Ward, J.H. "Microcomputer Use at Wilcox High School." *California Library Educators Association Journal* 3:12-14, Spring 1980.
149. "Age of Anxiety: Group Therapy Studies Show it Has Little Value in Helping People Contend With Stress." *Wall Street Journal,* Apr. 16, 1979.
150. "Many Executives Complain of Stress But Few Want Less Pressured Jobs." *Wall Street Journal,* Sept. 29, 1982.
151. Ward, Pearl L. "The Librarian's Personality; Or More Than Scraps of Information," in *The School Media Center,* compiled by Pearl L. Ward and Robert Beacon. Metuchen, N.J.: Scarecrow Press, 1973.
152. Ward, Pearl L. "Teacher/Librarian Relations." *Catholic Library World* 50:132-34, October 1978.
153. Wassmer, Arthur C. *Making Contact.* New York: Dial Press, 1978.
154. Watt, Ann Stewart. "School Libraries and Black American Children," in *Handbook of Black Librarianship.* Littleton, Colo.: Libraries Unlimited, 1977.
155. Weigel, Randy, and Pinsky, Sheldon. "Managing Stress: A Model for the Human Resource Staff." *Personnel Administrator* 27: 56-60, February 1982.
156. Wheeler, Ladd, et al. *Interpersonal Influence.* Boston: Allyn and Bacon, 1978.
157. Winfield, Tom. "A Crystal Ball for Educators." *American Education* 15:6-9, July 1979.
158. Wood, Johanna S. "Media Programs in Open Space Schools." *School Media Quarterly* 4:205-14, Spring 1976.
159. Wood, Johanna S. "The Role of Media Specialists in the Curriculum Process." *School Library Journal* 23:20-21,

September 1976.
160. Woods, L.B., and Salvatore, Lucy. "Self-censorship in Collection Development by High School Library Media Specialists." *School Library Media Quarterly*, 9:102-08, Winter 1981.
161. Worshel, Stephen, and Cooper, Joel. *Understanding Social Psychology*. Homewood, Ill.: The Dorsey Press, 1979.
162. Zamora, Ramon. "Future Play." *ComputerTown USA* 3:6, May/June, 1982.
163. Zamora, Ramon. "Recess: A Column on Informal Education." *ComputerTown USA*, January 1982.

Index

Administrator relations, 38-44
  impediments, 43
  principal's expectations, 41-42
Censorship of materials, 57-58
  school district policy on selection of materials, Appendix E
Change, 1-2; 62-66
  planned change, 63
  mandated change, 63
  forces against change, 63-64
  changes in operation at present and to come, 68-71
Child needs
  chart, Appendix C
Citizen's request for reconsideration of a book, Appendix E
Communication, 34-36
Computers, 67-76
  problems, 74-76
  sources for software evaluations, Appendix F
  stress reduction, 72-76
Coping
  internal factors, 18-19
  external factors 19-20
  employer sponsored programs, 26-33
  information for the mentally and physically handicapped and cultural and ethnic minority students, Appendix G
  coping strategies for pressure, 10-13
  students with behavior problems, 85-86
  change, 22-25; 64-65
  technological change, 72-76
  culturally and ethnically different students, 79-80
  curriculum changes, 92-94
  changed financial support, 100-104
  student body changes, 78-86
  mentally and physically handicapped, 81-84
Creed for working with students, 52-53
Cultural and ethnic minority students, 78-80
  materials, Appendix G
  stress reduction, 79-80
Curriculum and school organization changes, 88-95
  future curriculum, 90-91
  planning curriculum units, Appendix H
Employer sponsored stress reduction programs, 26-33
  guidelines, 27
  model stress management plan, 26-33
Financial support changes, 96-105

causes of decreased support, 99-100
social and political trends af—fecting support, 96-99
stress reduction 100-105
Future society projections, 89-90
Interpersonal relations, 34-37
Leadership
 guidelines for group leadership, Appendix I
Lobbying, 100
Materials selection policy, Appendix E
Mentally and physically handicapped students, 80-84
 materials, Appendix G
 stress reduction, 81-84
Parent and community members relations, 57-61
 stress reduction, 58-59
Pressure, 10-15
 sources, 14-15
 stress reduction, 13-14
Principal-library media specialist conferences simulated, 11-12
Principal-library media specialist relations, 38-44
 Test, Appendix B
Principal's expectations for library media staff, 41-43
Relaxation therapy, Appendix A
Social and political trends affecting funding for public education, 99-100
Society
 predictions for future, 89-90
Stress
 definition, 5
 stress reduction
  employer sponsored programs, 26-33
 summary of strategies, 106-107
Stress-creating situations, 43-44; 49-50; 54-55; 60-61; 77; 86-87; 94-95; 104-105
Stress management plan
 guidelines, 27
 model, 31-33
Stress reduction, 17-25. See also Coping
 summary of strategies, 106-107
Stress symptoms, 7-8
Stressful work conditions, 6-7
Student body changes, 78-87
 stress reduction, 79-80; 81-84; 85-86
Student developmental needs, 51-52
 chart, Appendix C
Student misbehavior, 84
 stress reduction, 85-87
Student relations, 51-55; 78-87
 culturally and ethnically different, 79-80
 mentally and physically handicapped, 80-84
 students with unacceptable standards of behavior, 84-86
 stress reduction, 52-54; 79-80; 81-84; 85-86
Support systems, 9-10; 19; 11-13
Teacher centers, 24
Teacher relations, 45-50
 suggestions for good relations, 47-49
Technological change, 67-77
 problems associated with new technologies, 74-76
 stress reduction, 72-76
Volunteers
 school district volunteer program and ethics for volunteers, Appendix D